The Dark Secrets of Rebecca Marie

By R.M. Mendez

V.6.0

ISBN # 978-1450516570

Made in USA

Available on Kindle and Paperback

Introduction

Emotionally, scars are deep with abused children. Such children grow up to be abusers out of bitterness or they become ongoing victims. People from all lifestyles notice when a child is different. They see when a child is downhearted, bruised, hungry, and frightened. Yet, they walk passed with that look of pity, without a word, without the tiniest offering of help. Most people do not want to get involved fearing their interference will bring them trouble. Alternatively, they feel it is simply not their business... I hate to say it but some people just do not care.

In addition, child services programs fail miserably from being under-staffed and overworked. The courts in their wisdom make every effort to keep children with their biological parents. Child abusers are great actors giving convincing speeches despite the evidence. A plea of not guilty followed by a promise to attend counseling is all that is needed to send a child back to the hell of which they came. Nevertheless, I have a great respect for social workers and admire their efforts.

This story is about true accounts of how I dealt with abuse throughout my life. Some memories are simply too painful to write about and other memories are lost to me. There are times that seem like blank voids that I cannot recall. My family told me that I was a chronic sleepwalker, so severe at times I would leave the house and roam the streets. Therefore, they installed locks, out of my reach to ensure I remained in the house. I do not write about those events, as I have no memory of them. All that I know about my sleepwalking was my mother accusing me of speaking in tongues and being possessed by the devil. I received many beatings for the purposes of driving the devil out of me.

My life has been one of many secrets, fears and a desperate need for escape. At my present age of fifty-four, it is difficult to recapture every detail of events from my past. Therefore, in telling this story, some dates could be wrong and dialog exchanged not repeated word for word. I will write dialog as I remember it or as I feel it was said according to the event. Some people I have left out because of their minor role in my life, it just does not seem important. I write about the people who had the most impact on me. Keep in mind that I am writing from my point of view and that will include imaginary friends, dreams, and inner-feelings. Out of respect for my sons, I only pass lightly over their lives and focus only on my experiences.

From a very early age, I kept my sanity by writing

in journals. When I was too young to spell words, I drew pictures. I would steal my sister's crayons and go through the garbage in search of paper. I desperately drew pictures of my mother with sharp teeth and long bloody fingernails. I would be creative in hiding my journals and at times destroyed them for fear SHE might find them and I would then suffer dire consequences.

Nervous, grossly underweight, and longing for love and acceptance I created imaginary friends, so real to me at times my imaginary friends became my salvation. I suppose, some people would say I lost my mind, plagued with sleepwalking, nightmares, and trouble distinguishing reality from fantasy.

After writing a poem about my childhood, (poem is at end of this story) I suddenly had a need to share my past with my new husband. However, he simply could not understand and felt I was dwelling on the past, thinking that was not good for me. However, as I continually relive my past in my dreams the need to speak out brought me to write this memoir. It is surprisingly healing to let out all my secrets. Moreover, I began to realize that this story might help other victims heal too.

I of course changed the names of people and places for obvious reasons. Estranged from my family, I did not want to stir up trouble or upset anyone at this late date. It is not my desire to seek revenge. My heart is filled with forgiveness and pity for my tormentors because they now have their demons to deal with. Their ignorance and sense of denial are not worth allowing bitterness to consume me. In reinventing myself, happiness is all that matters to me.

Chapter 1

Eddie-Boy

I was born in 1954 in the great era of Rock n' Roll. Teenagers were dancing to the tunes of Buddy Holly, Jerry Lee Lewis, and Elvis Presley. Adults were in top form as Latin Swing was all the rage. Television was new and had everyone's attention as they watched the Honeymooners and I love Lucy. Post World War II, it was a time of prosperity in which so many were now living the American dream. Most families owned their own home and nearly everyone had a car in their driveway. It was a simple time of trust and family. Lifc was good.

My mother was a German immigrant. My father came from Cuba, proudly becoming an American citizen after serving in World War II. He was a hero who earned two purple hearts while fighting the enemy in Japan. When he returned to the states, he became a merchant marine and world traveler.

Through a mutual friend, my father met my mother. When he looked at her, he saw a red-haired beauty with bewitching green eyes. However, all my mother could see in him was how freely and generously he handed out money without a care. Going off to sea for months at a time, he would dock in ports with a salary paid out to him that was to say the least . . . impressive.

Going against her upbringing and needing a home for her three children my mother spun her web. She was mean and bitter, a single parent in an era that saw it socially unacceptable to be a divorced woman. My mother planned to correct her situation at any cost to gain the respect of the community, even if it meant marrying a Cuban . . . a man of ethnic origin . . . a man of color. Her goal was to own a home, a car and to build security for her three precious children.

At twenty-eight years old, my father married and became the stepfather of three children, which I believe my father happily accepted because he loved children. Within a short time, my father purchased a home for his new family and saw to all their needs. They were the perfect family, or so it seemed.

My mother was a vampire, feeding on the love my father felt for her. This was my beginnings; was I cursed? Did I just have bad luck? On the other hand, maybe reincarnation is true and this life was my punishment for sins long ago committed? There are no answers to those questions, yet, the never-ending question echoes in my mind, “Why me?”

My parents argued bitterly over money and her need to be in complete control. Her children spoiled and self-centered was also the cause of my parent's bitter exchange of words. After four years of unhappiness, disappointment, and heartbreak, my father reached his boiling point. He walked out of the house and slammed the door after a violent argument with my mother. I knew I was in serious trouble at that very moment. I was only four years old, but I knew my dark days would now begin. I turned and faced my mother with tears of fear in my eyes. The look on her face spoke to me without words. I could see even at my age that she felt consumed with hatred as she now stared me down. Oh, why did my father leave me behind?

That night in the cold, dirty garage, I entered my prison for the first time. What was my crime… was I simply born bad or, was it that I simply am me? I now realize that I was my mother's shame. My hair and eyes dark in color, my skin not as fair as hers made me appear deformed and ugly in her eyes. I was a heavy burden for her to deal with, but at four years old, I did not understand her frame of mind. I thought I was just bad. Therefore, to gain her love and acceptance all I ever said for every situation, trying my hardest to please was, "I'm sorry. I'll be good."

At the tender age of four years old, I had no sense of time. It seemed like such a long time since my father walked out the door, without turning back. How long had it been, was it hours, days, or weeks? I do not know. I waited in great anticipation for his return in hopes that he would rescue me. However, he did not return and now I faced my first real punishment. I was alone, no means of defense, no escape . . . little more than a trapped animal.

I cannot remember what I did to upset my mother to such an extent. I must have done something terrible. She hit me repeatedly with her open hand. The crack against my flesh was utterly frightening. I flew this way and that as each strike seemed to lift me and send me tumbling across the room. I found it strange how my cries sounded to me, my own voice foreign to me. My cries of terror and pain filled the room.

Finally, she stopped to catch her breath. She was panting from exhaustion and spouting garbled obscenities at me. I felt numb and was not sure if I was asleep or awake. I felt a strange numbness. Yet, I could feel the cold of the concrete against my flesh. Moreover, try as I might I could not open my eyes.

Suddenly, the door slammed with a great explosion and brought me back to my senses. I lay sprawled on the floor. I wanted to move but I could not move a muscle. I touched my face and it felt so strange, the skin tight and sticky. I moaned. My moans echoed in my ears. I had no real concept of death, yet I thought I was dead.

A tiny voice whispered in my ear, "I'll take care of you." I tried to turn my head to see who spoke to me. Was I dreaming? I began to sob with great heaves welling from within my chest. The tears that now rolled out of my eyes stung brutally on my cut lips making me cry even more. Moments later, I moved into a fetal position for comfort. Pain now found a home in my body. I looked up, my eyes nearly blinded me from the swelling . . . I saw a dark blur, trying hard to see as I slowly began to focus a little, I saw a shape . . . a thin boy. He said, "I'm Eddie-boy. You'll be all right. I'll take care of you."

I wanted to speak to him but my sobbing now made my body shake uncontrollably. My back felt tight and painful. The tears running over my cut lips felt like fire and now my head and eyes were throbbing to the point of madness. I was beyond speech, beyond reason only the pain and my sobbing filled my mind.

I felt Eddie-boy hold me and give me comfort. The tighter he held me the more I cried. Was I dreaming? I felt his heart beat under my ear. I think I was holding onto him and not wanting him to let me go.

Suddenly, I felt what I thought was huge, thick drool coming from my mouth. When to my horror I realized it was BLOOD! I mumbled hoping that from some magic force my father or God could hear me, "Da- Da-ddy, I wa-wa-nt my Da-Da-ddy." Speaking was a struggle as I stuttered.

Eddie-boy said, "He cannot come to help you. It's just you and me." I stuttered, "I wa-wa-nt my Da- Da- ddy." I always stuttered horribly with each word, another deformity to all the many flaws I possessed.

Eddie-boy placed a cold, wet, dirty washcloth to my lips and held it there or, maybe I held it there, I am not sure. Who was this little boy that came to help me?

Over the weeks or months that followed, (I do not really know how much time passed) I lived in a state of daily beatings, denied food, soap, or any basic needs. The hardest part was the never-ending desire for food. All I could think about was food.

Eddie-boy was my constant companion now. He taught me to survive by eating out of the trash and he always reminded me to drink plenty of water. The washbasin in the garage always had a constant drip, drip from the faucet. I cupped my hands under it the way Eddie-boy showed me, then waited for my cupped hands to fill so I could consume the delicious water. It is amazing how flavors were so robust for me, even water.

Eddie-boy was a genius for ways to survive and the best part is nobody could see him but me. Sometimes, when my beatings were worst than usual, Eddie-boy would enter with friends. He once told me that he and his friends use to get beat by their parents, too. However, their parents could not hurt them anymore. I never questioned where Eddie-boy and his friends came from or how they could disappear and reappear from the wall. I did not care; all that mattered is that they were here with me.

One day, I sat huddled in a corner for warmth within my sleeping bag, when I heard a care drive-up. I held my breath in fear as I pressed my body against the wall hoping to disappear the way Eddie-boy did. Try as I might, I remained. I heard the car door shut . . . Then, I heard my mother's familiar heels clip-clop on the walkway up to the house. The front door clicked as she opened it followed by the thunderous crashing slam of the door. Then, my mother's footfalls approaching sounded like a bomb ticking as tears now streamed from my eyes. Terror gripped me as I felt my spine tighten, my mouth dry, adrenalin pumping through my heart as I wondered if she would kill me this time.

My stare fixed on the door as I watched the handle turn . . . the door flew open and all I could think to say, in a desperate attempt to save myself, "Mama! I'm sorry!"

She glared at me with unimaginable hate as she spat out through clenched teeth, "You will NEVER call me Mama! My name is Nancy! Never call me Mama again. I am stuck with you and you will shut your mouth and do as I say. I hate you . . . you are nothing . . . no better than a gutter rat!"

I boldly stuttered as my body shook, "I wa- wa-nt my Da- da-ddy."

She approached and I flinched expecting a slap. However, none came as she hissed, “He doesn’t want you. He knows you will grow up to be a dirty little slut! Go wash your face I need to take a picture of you.”

My mother grabbed me, shoved me over to the washbasin, and turned on the cold water. I trembled in fear, confused as to what a Slut was and why my father did not want me. He always said that he loved me.

Suddenly, I heard Eddie-boy whisper in my ear, “Hurry and wash your face. Do as she says, quickly. It’s Christmas! Maybe she wants you to go inside the house. I’ll bet there are hot buttery mash potatoes.”

I glanced at my mother and took notice that she could not see Eddie-boy or hear him. My mother was watching me with such cold unfeeling eyes. I turned to the washbasin envisioning hot steaming mash potatoes drowning in gravy. I imagined a hot cup of cocoa and it made my heart hammer in anticipation. I was so hungry and could not remember the last time I ate.

I splashed my face and scrubbed it good with the washcloth. Then, I turned and she roughly ran a brush through my hair yanking my head back with each pull. My mother handed me a white night gown and gestured to me with a wave of her hand to put it on. I put the new nightgown on and could not help but to smile. She glared at me, infuriated by my smile, which quickly faded as I hung my head with down-cask eyes.

My mother shoved me toward the steps up to the kitchen. As I passed through the doorway, the warmth of the house seemed to engulf me. It felt so good to feel warm. I could smell all the glorious delights of food. I felt my face flush hot wondering how I was managing to move my legs. I felt almost in a dream-state and wondered if I was dreaming. My mother shoved me toward a chair and handed me a warm steaming cup. I looked into it and she shrieked at me to hurry and drink it. I took a sip of the broth and nearly gulped it all down. It was so delicious.

After I put the cup down, my mother now guided me to the living room. My mouth watered at the sight of COOKIES, CAKE, and HOT COCOA on the coffee table where my siblings happily sat enjoying a Christmas feast, wearing their new holiday clothes. There were presents throughout the room, most were open revealing beautiful dolls of every size, a china tea set, a toy baby carriage, and many lovely clothes laid about.

As wonderful at it all looked, the only interest I had was the mashed-potatoes all buttery and hot as my stomach growled. My brother sat taking in large spoonfuls dripping in gravy. My lower lip quivered, longing for a taste . . . just a small taste. I seemed to go deaf and time came to a stand still for me as I looked at the food. . . . I held my breath as my stare remained fixed on my brother, watching the spoon slip between his lips and into his mouth . . .

I was deaf to my mother's scolding when suddenly; an ear-piercing slap took my attention away from the savory food on display as my body went flying and crashed against the wall. My sister grabbed my wrist and yanked me up to my feet as she ordered, "Open the present, and look at Mama!"

Shaken, I could hardly think straight. I put my hands on the package and looked at my mother who held a camera. The flash of the camera went off in a bright yellow blur.

Suddenly, my sister whisked me away and shoved back into the cold garage. I looked up at the spider webs fearing the ghastly creatures. Heaving with a great sigh, I crawled back to my corner and back to my sleeping bag. I looked around thinking the spiders would surely crawl on me and bite me if I closed my eyes. I began to sob, pleading to God to send my daddy to save me. I felt the new nightgown I still wore wondering why she let me keep it. It was so soft and pretty but offered no warmth.

Eddie-boy came up to me, smiling. "You can still have mash potatoes tonight. Just wait until Nancy cleans the kitchen and puts the trash out. You and I will have our own Christmas feast."

Eddie-boy waved his hand and children came out of the wall. All the children were thin and pale, in tattered clothes and all of them smiled happily at me. They gave me a feeling of belonging. I shivered from the cold but a little girl came up to me and took me into her embrace.

We all huddled together, waited, and watched the door in anticipation of the kitchen trash. Although, I do not remember the trash ever being put out, sure enough late that night Eddie-boy and the children shared our own Christmas feast from a shining, silver trash can. We enjoyed turkey, mash potatoes, and other mysterious delights that were in the garbage can. We laughed and giggled as we gobbled up the food making a mess on our faces.

That night Eddie-boy and his friends did not leave me. Instead, we all lay down together and slept soundly. I felt so warm and cozy. My tummy felt full as joy filled my heart even though tears flooded my eyes. I could not help but to think, why did Nancy want to take a picture of me in front of the presents? Later, I found out that my father sent me all the presents and he requested a picture of me opening them. Why did he send me presents when what I needed was for him to rescue me?

Chapter 2

Some Days were Nice

The winter of 1959 was long, bitterly cold and I was starving to death. I was often ill. Those nights when fever consumed me they allowed me to sleep in the house. After I felt a little better, Nancy sent me back to the garage. My body was always in pain, with wounds that took a long time to heal. I could only console myself by the joy of Eddie-Boy's company. How would I have dealt with it all, without my dear little friend?

Laundry-day, my mother spent in the garage putting the clothes through the wringer washer. She hung the clothes up to dry on clotheslines within the garage. This meant I spent most of the day in her company. I cowered in the corner trying to make myself invisible. She would curse at me and scold me for simply being there. Why did she hate me so much?

She made me take my shoes and socks off and sit on a footstool within the garage. I would have to sit on my hands with my bare feet on the cold concrete floor. If I moved or made a noise, I was certain to get a fierce slap across my face or a smack upside my head. After a while, my feet hurt from the bitter cold and my hands became numb from sitting on them for such a long time. My back ached, something awful as the unbearable urge to urinate nearly made me feel ill. I was so cold that I trembled, clenching my teeth hard so as not to let them chatter, fearing another blow to my face and head if I made noise. My stomach growled as the visions in my mind filled with all my favorite foods. I let out inner cries, *Help! Please help me God... send my Daddy to save me,* was all I repeated within my thoughts. However, my pleas and prayers went unanswered as I began to imagine my Daddy might be dead, maybe his ship sank.

Suddenly, my mother pulled me up to my feet. After sitting for so long my legs had fallen asleep and could not support my weight. I felt as if darkness came and went, feeling confused and wondering if I was dreaming. I suppose I moaned. I do not remember if I spoke but not being able to resist any longer I urinated in my pants, making Nancy angrier. She grabbed a short piece of clothesline, began whipping my legs, and ordered me to walk around in a circle. I stumbled many times. My legs stung at first from being whipped but after a few moments, the pain took over my entire body as I forced myself to walk around in a circle. Tears poured down my face as I tried to obey Nancy's commands. I found myself jumping up and down, I suppose she ordered that of me too. I could not seem to hear yet obeyed every command.

Finally, she broke the spell of madness with laughter. She walked up the steps to the kitchen where she slammed the door behind her. I collapsed panting for air and feeling a cold clammy sweat consume my body. I was so thirsty, my mouth felt dry like cotton. Eddie-Boy rushed over to me and quickly put my socks back on my feet for warmth. He guided me over to my sleeping bag where I curled up trying to find a degree of warmth. I think I cried myself to sleep. I woke when it was dark and I could hear talking from within the kitchen.

Eddie-boy told me, "They are getting dinner ready. Maybe you will get some food tonight. You were a good girl and did exactly what Nancy told you, after all."

My head throbbed terribly and my left eye felt swollen and shut. Nancy had struck me upside the head many times throughout the day, obviously injuring my eye. Suddenly, the kitchen door opened and Sam said, "Get in the house, pig!"

I stood up and walked over to the steps where he repeated, "Get in the house, pig... Jesus god, you stink!"

I walked slowly up the steps and entered the kitchen feeling the warmth coming from the oven. I could smell the glorious fragrance of fresh baked bread. Ellen, Hester, and Sam held their nose gesturing that I stunk. Nancy stood with her hands on her hips and just stared at me for a moment. I dare not move or make a sound so I just stood with downcast eyes waiting for the next command.

Nancy ordered, "You need a bath. Go sit in the hallway next to the bathroom door and wait your turn."

I did not realize that I smelled. I had not seen my reflection so I had no idea what the bruising on my face looked like or the extent of my injuries. It felt so go to be in the warm house. I went over and sat on the floor, next to the bathroom door as Nancy entered the bathroom first to take a bath.

From where I sat, I could see the TV and that was a nice treat but for some reason everything looked blurry. After a while, my body finally felt warm but the pain now became near unbearable. My legs felt tingly and my head ached. I touched the side of my swollen face in hopes to stop the throbbing.

Eddie-Boy walked up and sat next to me. "It's warm and soon you'll have a bath and maybe a hot dinner. Don't think so much about the pain you feel."

Eddie-Boy was such a comfort to me. I leaned my head on his shoulder, or maybe it was the wall and then closed my eyes.

I woke when Nancy walked out of the bathroom. The fragrance that followed was heavenly. Next, Ellen entered the bathroom for her bath. My headache was now so terrible I could not even pinpoint the spot that ached more. I tried to swallow but my mouth was too dry.

Sam and Hester were in the living room watching the Wonderful World of Disney on TV. Normally, I would have been thrilled to watch TV, especially Disney. However, I simply could not keep my eyes open. Strangely, even though the house was warm I began to feel cold and clammy and my eyes were burning. I dozed off again and woke when Ellen called out for Hester's turn to take a bath. This was certainly a wild event as Hester hissed and protested, refusing a bath which was normal for her. I often heard her protesting bath time with a temper-tantrum.

Nancy stormed into the living room with a belt in hand. "Get in that bathroom and wash your filthy body... NOW!"

Once Hester took notice of the belt, she ran to the bathroom and shut the door. Nancy walked up to me with a curious look on her face. She squatted down and put her hand to my forehead. Then, she stood towering over me and just stared at me. Maybe she spoke; if she did, I could not hear her. I saw her walk over to Ellen who then hurried out of the room. She returned with garments in her hand and handed them to Nancy who sat and just watched me. My eyes shut again and I suppose I fell off to sleep.

Suddenly, Nancy shouted at Hester to hurry which brought Hester running out of the bathroom, in her pajamas with her wet hair tied back in a ponytail.

Nancy then walked up to me and grunted, “Your turn, get in there!”

I tried to stand but could not. I am not sure if Eddie-boy or Nancy helped me up. Once in the bathroom, she ordered me to remove all my clothes except for my panties. Nancy had a strict rule that girls never got completely naked because it was a sin. Standing in my panties, I turned and looked at the filthy bath water.

Nancy always bathed with bath oils and her constant need to economize meant we had to share bath wate to keep the water bill low. Yes, after Nancy had her bath, Ellen, Hester and I took turns using the SAME water. By the time, it was my turn the oil caused a dark greasy ring around the tub, soap-scum, and body filth floated in the water in a very uninviting manner and yes, by now the water was COLD. Before I could react, she pushed me over to the sink and made me stand on the stool.

Nancy put my head under the faucet in the sink to wash my hair. She was brutal as she washed and scrubbed my filthy hair. Then, she combed it out pulling my head back. My hair was curly so a mess of tangles after a wash. When she was done she tied my hair into a ponytail. Nancy then scooped me up and placed me in that disgusting bath water. It felt like Nancy scrubbed me nearly to the bone. I do not remember all the details of the entire bath experience; it was as if I was drifting in and out of sleep.

Next, I found myself at the kitchen table. My head felt like it weighed a ton and sleep was heavily consuming me. Ellen put a plate of beef stew and a fresh baked dinner roll in front of me. "EAT!" snapped Ellen.

I felt so tired and could not remember when I ate last. I picked up the fresh baked dinner roll and dipped into the stew then held it up so Eddie-Boy could take the first bite. I took a bite feeling the dinner roll melt in my mouth. It was so delicious.

However, as I looked at the stew I felt like vomiting. I think I ate the bread; my mind seemed to shut off because the next thing I remember I was in bed. The room was dark and it appeared as if everyone in the house was asleep. My stomach was churning and I feared I might vomit. I got up and ran to the bathroom, but no vomit came forth. There I lay on the bathroom rug and waited but the feeling to vomit passed. I got up and took a drink from the sink then tiptoed back to bed.

I felt a little better understanding I was very ill. I slept a long time undisturbed. When I woke again, it was dark. Having lost track of time I thought it was the night when Ellen walked into the room and said, "Oh, so you are still alive. Get up, it's dinner time."

I sat up and felt much better. Ellen gave me a robe and slippers and I followed her to the kitchen where I ate until my heart was content. By the next morning, I felt as good as new and nearly happy.

"What are you so cheerful about? You are the devil... your eyes are black and evil. Get in that garage and pray God will forgive you your sins," demanded Nancy.

Shocked and not really understanding what Nancy meant, I foolishly protested, "I am not the devil... I don't want to go to the garage!"

Big mistake! Nancy stood up, grabbed my arm lifting me off the floor, and proceeded to storm through the kitchen and literary tossed me into the garage. I flew like a rag doll against the laundry hamper. Nancy walked toward me with a look of murder in her eyes when she heard the phone ring. She turned and Ellen called out, "The phone... it's that man... Bill, he wants to talk to you." Nancy smiled and ran off to answer the phone forgetting all about me.

Eddie-boy walked over to me after Ellen shut the door and said, "One day, you and I will leave this place. We'll have our own home and eat all our favorite foods, every day. We'll sleep in beds with clean sheets and always feel warm."

After that day, for the most part I was alone in the garage. Now and then, Ellen would give me a dinner plate. I was not eating every day and certainly not three meals a day. I do not know how often I ate each week but it was not enough. The cold at times was more than I could bear and I became creative to keep warm using the dirty laundry, newspaper, and magazines for my makeshift bed. When the wind blew, it came right through the side slits in the garage door and so I crammed newspaper in the cracks. Since Nancy kept the garage door locked at all times, no one complained about the newspapers I used to create a seal.

Winter finally gave way to spring, which was wet making the garage very damp. At this time, Nancy allowed me to sleep a little more often in the house, although, if I said or did anything that upset her I was back in the garage.

Finally, summer was in the air and warmth was now a constant. I loved summer. Nancy allowed me to go out to the backyard and there I could lie in the grass and soak in the sun as I daydreamed of better places and happy times of love that awaited me in the future.

It was at this time that I attempted to start a journal. Of course, I could not write but I stole some of Hester's old broken crayons and dug paper from the trash; old envelopes, paper bags, and such. I began drawing pictures of Nancy, with bloody claws, sharp teeth, and horns. I drew pictures of her special children eating and watching TV. I laid out all that I saw, feared, and experienced in my simple drawings. It seemed to bring me a sense of relief. I would draw myself looking beautiful, with blond hair although my hair was dark brown. I would color in blue eyes instead of my dark black eyes. I would draw myself wearing pretty dresses and a big smile on my face. Eddie-boy gave me praise for my artistic flare and he promised me that one day I would be beautiful, happy, and loved.

At first, I did not notice but since Ellen was on summer vacation from school and home all the time, I nearly never saw Nancy. I do not know where she went but I did not care so long as she was gone. Ellen was mean to me too, but for the most part only in a verbal way. The fact is it was better for me when Ellen was in charge. Ellen was obsessed with cleanliness and therefore, she did make me take a bath a few times a week in clean water. It must have been very difficult for Ellen when Nancy was home and made her take a bath in dirty water.

Ellen did not care where I was during the day so long as I was not in her presence. In Ellen's care, she allowed to eat a little more often. I know she was afraid that I would get sick in her care and often scolded me, "Eat, I don't want you getting sick!" She yelled at me, and called me clumsy and stupid. She was hateful to me but it was still better with her than with Nancy. Ellen never beat me and for that, I was grateful.

Ellen was a teenager and Hester about twelve years old. Since Ellen was in charge, she always had her girlfriends over to visit. They smoked cigarettes and invited boys over. They played records, danced, and even kissed the boys.

Ellen did not want me to see their activities because she was afraid I would tell when Nancy got home. Nancy forbade such things as smoking and boys in the house. Therefore, she opened the side gate, removed a red tricycle from the shed, and told me I could ride it. She allowed me to go outside to play with the other children!

I rode off on the tricycle, feeling so free and happy. However, I had no idea that my appearance was quite contrary to the other children. I was deathly skinny, my clothes old and worn-out and the kids began to call me Raggedy-Ann. I was cleaner now so I suppose I did not stink but the name-calling was hurtful. I began to stay to myself to avoid the mean kids who hated me for some unknown reason.

I rode my bike up the sidewalk to the north then down all the way to the south end of the block with Eddie-Boy on the handlebars. He kept an eye on which house was mine, since they were all pretty much the same. We were worried about getting lost. It was a wonderful day for Eddie-boy and me. After a while, the children pretty much ignored me.

When, I heard Ellen call me, I raced my bike back to the front porch with a smile fixed on my face. She looked at me strangely for a moment then calmly said, “Put the bike back in the shed. It’s time for dinner.”

I nodded and raced my bike around back and parked the bike in the shed and closed the door. I took in a deep breath and whispered, “Thank you God.”

Once inside, Ellen made me wash my hands and face then sit at the dinner table. She had warmed up a can of chicken noodle soup and served me the soup with crackers. I gobbled it up being sure to hand Eddie-Boy crackers and spoonfuls of soup. I felt that life could not be better. When I was done, Ellen told me to go to the bedroom and get ready for bed. I felt wide-awake and had no desire to sleep. Nevertheless, I obeyed so as not to upset Ellen and ruin the day. Not all my days were miserable... some days were very nice.

Chapter 3

He's Back!

Autumn came and now Nancy was home all the time. She spent lots of time at the sewing machine making clothes for herself, Hester, Ellen and even me. In the garage, the nights were cold but the days were warm. I kept thinking what fun it was to ride the bike and how much I missed it. I did not care that Ellen called me stupid and clumsy or that Sam would call me nigger or pig. I enjoyed riding the bike and had fun times with Eddie-boy. Eddie-boy always assured me that we would get another day to ride the bikc.

Many months passed since my father left and I gave up on him ever returning. After waiting for so long, I assumed he was dead. I would never believe what Nancy told me about him. My father loved me, and if he did not return, it simply was because he was dead.

I sat huddled in the corner of the garage, in my dirty old sleeping bag. I was only five years old but I was already daydreaming of running away from home. Suddenly, SHE stood at the door and just stared at me with that evil glare. She grabbed a kitchen chair and walked up to me. My automatic response was to shield my face, which only made her angry and smack me upside the head. Nancy held a drink in her hand as she started her speech.

"When you are asked how you are doing, you will respond with 'I am doing well, thank you.' If you are asked why you are so skinny or why you do not eat more you are to respond with, 'I don't like to eat.' If you are asked if your mother feeds you, you are to respond with 'yes, she makes me delicious meals but I am just not hungry.' Nancy paused then continued, "If you are taken out to eat you will NOT finish the food on your plate. You will take a few bites and then say you are full! Do you understand?"

The truth was I did not understand at all and just looked at her blankly. She smacked me a few times and the drilling began for what seemed like hours. Nancy forced me to repeat rehearsed lines of speech. If I stuttered too much or got the sentence wrong, I was smacked, hard. I grew tired and felt hungry as the drilling continued with only small pauses while Nancy went to refill her drink. Eddie-boy stood by and whispered in my ear, each line to be sure I got it right and avoided another smack.

Finally, pleased with my rehearsed performance, Nancy stood up and returned to the kitchen slamming the door behind her as she always did. I sat for a while wondering what that was all about but then felt too tired to really care. I lied down and fell asleep.

At first light, Nancy rushed me to the

bathroom for a bath, in filthy used water... of course. Then, I sat on a tall stool as Nancy proceeded to style my hair into finger curls, just like Shirley Temple. She was mean as she yanked my head back and nearly jammed bobby pins in my head while warning me that I better not cry and make my face all red.

When, my hair was finished she sprayed it heavily with hair spray. Then, I was marched to the bedroom where a beautiful dress of blue with a big white lace collar awaited me. I wore white tights and the prettiest lacy socks with black patent-leather shoes. Ellen put white gloves on me and handed me a cute little purse with a lacy white handkerchief in it. Nancy always stressed the importance of gloves and a purse to be proper for a lady. She had many rules on proper grooming and behavior for a lady.

Eddie-boy smiled as he said, "You look beautiful!"

Nancy looked at me and I swear she almost smiled and nearly agreed with Eddie-boy even though she could not hear him or see him.

Then, the drilling started with rehearsed lines she wanted me to memorize. I looked at my white gloves and my pretty, black shoes and thought *I must be dreaming. I wonder why I get to wear these beautiful clothes. If this is a dream, I hope I never wake up.*

Suddenly Sam called out, "He's here!"

Nancy looked at me and warned, "You better say what I told you to say word for word!"

She then yanked on my hand and told me to go out to the car and mind my manners. I did not know what to make about what was happening. Why did she want me to go out to the car alone? I slowly went out the door and walked down the steps to the driveway. There was a black car parked. I stood for a moment and watched the car door open. My jaw dropped in utter surprise as I saw my father step out of the car with a big smile. We just looked at each other for a few moments. He broke the silence as his smiled faded. "Don't you remember me, TeeTee?"

He always called me TeeTee. I felt overwhelmed as I thought, *He's alive, he's alive! He finally came to rescue me!*"

I wanted to run into his arms and feel him lift me and hold me to his heart but I shyly replied, "Yes, I remember you." He seemed disappointed with me because I just stood there like a dummy with no love to offer. My father took my hand, walked me to the passenger side of the car, and opened the door. I crawled into the seat and sat with my hands holding my purse, void of emotion. I wanted to hug him and never let go. I wanted to tell him that I loved him but no words came from my mouth. What was wrong with me?

We drove off as my father started conversation telling me, "You're so skinny, do you get enough to eat?" And so, started my reply of rehearsed answers, to the letter. My father glanced at me as he drove making me think he did not believe me. We got on the freeway and drove for a while. I looked out the window enjoying the car ride. Despite my cold emotionless expression, I was having the time of my life. I looked at my purse and at my shoes and felt life could not be better. I glanced at my Daddy and imagined he was taking me to his home, where I would always dress pretty and be his precious little girl.

We parked at a restaurant and we entered the building where friendly Chinese people greeted my Daddy. He spoke just like them; I had no idea what they were saying. It was obvious that they were long time friends of his.

The older lady hugged me and brought out a booster chair for me whereupon I sat as a feast. I was so hungry my mouth watered. First served was a cup of soup, which I gobbled up. My Daddy, whispered, "Eat slowly, TeeTee."

I looked at him and remembered what Nancy told me. She told me if I go to a restaurant not to eat all the food and to act as if I was not hungry. Next served was vegetables with pork-fried rice and shrimp. At the time, I did not know the name of the food but the smell was heavenly. I looked at my Daddy and said, "I'm not hungry, Daddy."

With a look of concern, my Daddy said, "Eat TeeTee, you are so skinny. Please eat for me."

I wanted desperately to please him therefore; I did eat and ate and ate. The nice Chinese lady brought me a cup of tea, my very first cup of tea! I was so happy. I assumed it did not matter what Nancy told me, after all, I was not going to see her again. I was going to live with my Daddy now.

After lunch, we went to a park where my Daddy handed me a bag of bread and then handed me a small brown paper bag. He said, "The bread is for the ducks and I brought you this. A long time ago when you were about two years old, you forgot it at my father's house. He saved it for you."

I opened the bag and saw a small brown teddy bear with a cute plastic face. I smiled with delight as he continued to say, "Do you remember what you called it?" I shook my head and he continued, "You use to call it your MoMo." I smiled at my daddy as I embraced my MoMo. I was so happy.

We fed the ducks at the lake where I laughed with joy as the ducks followed me around. I was not void of emotion anymore. I was feeling loved and so wonderfully warm from within my heart. As it got late my Daddy said, "I better take you home."

I smiled as I ran to the car anxious to see my new home. We drove off and got on the freeway. I looked at my MoMo and my pretty purse. I clicked the heels of my shoes and glanced at my Daddy who smiled at me and blew me a kiss.

We drove and drove then turned off the freeway and down a familiar street. Oh my god! He was taking me back to Nancy! I begged and pleaded for him to take me with him. My Daddy said, "I don't know how to take care of a little girl, TeeTee. I have to go to work and..."

Panic overwhelmed me as I cried. He stopped in front the house and I threw my arms around his neck and pleaded desperately for him to take me with him. But, he honked the horn and out came Ellen. He said to me, "I have to go... I promise I'll be back soon to spend another day with you."

Ellen opened the car door as Nancy came out of the house. I got out of the car and so did my Daddy. Nancy looked at me with those hateful eyes and grunted, "What is that thing?"

I looked down at the teddy bear I held and replied, "MoMo"

My Daddy then said in a mean harsh voice to Nancy, "My father saved that bear for her and I expect you to let her keep it! If I find out that you took it away from her I swear I'll come back and..."

Nancy interrupted with her own angry voice, "What do you take me for, why would I take her toys away from her? Talk to me like that and you'll never see Rebecca Marie again!"

My Daddy then squatted down and gave me a hug, "I'll be back soon, I promise."

He got into the car and drove off. I hung my head wondering what was going to happen to me now. I ate the food at the restaurant against Nancy's orders. Surprisingly, Nancy just told me to go in the house and put my pajamas on.

Years later, I found out Nancy had to be careful where my Daddy was concerned to guarantee her child support and alimony checks. He was not just giving her money for my support. He also gave her money to run her house and feed all her children. During that year, I would get many visits from my Daddy and she knew he would be coming often so she had to ease up on me.

He returned every Sunday for a few months and we always went to the Chinese restaurant for lunch. My Daddy bought me many dresses and accessories. I was getting ready to start Kindergarten. Every visit ended with a flood of tears for my Daddy to take me away with him even though my situation was better at home now. Nevertheless, each time I he left me back in Nancy's care.

In public, Nancy played the part of my mother who cared about me. I went to Church now, every Sunday with Hester, Ellen and Nancy. I always wore pretty dresses to church so Nancy could present herself in the community as the devoted loving mother. I started school, wearing the nicest dresses anyone had ever seen, with lacy socks and pretty shoes. I loved my teacher who let me finger paint, color and sing songs. After milk and cookies the whole class laid out their blankets, my blanket was white and blue with clouds and baby angels. We would lay down for a nap while the teacher softly played the piano. Slowly, I began to gain weight and feel a little like I mattered although; they still addressed me at home by cruel names like stupid, clumsy and pig.

For the most part life was good and I shared all my happiness with Eddie-boy. However, little did I know it was only the calm before the storm.

Chapter 4

Help me God!

On Thanksgiving Day, my Daddy picked me up to take me to meet his family. Nancy grumbled, "It's Thanksgiving and I expect Rebecca Marie home for dinner!"

As always, my Daddy didn't even answer her. We drove off as I happily sat in the car with my cute little purse in hand. Tucked under my arm was my precious MoMo.

We went to my Aunt Louisa's house where it seemed to be busting with people in celebration. They allowed me to run and play with my cousins. It was such a fun day. We did not eat Turkey but strange foods and fish with fruit. It was all delicious. I was shocked when all the children sat to eat before the adults. In this house children were priority one. After we were finished with our Thanksgiving lunch, all the children went to the living room to watch the Thanksgiving Day parade on television. They served us cookies and hot chocolate as a TV snack.

The adults all gathered for their turn to eat. I could hear my aunts and uncles telling my Daddy how pretty I was and that I would probably grow up to be a movie star. I heard my Daddy tell my Aunt

Louisa, "Thank you for having Thanksgiving lunch for my TeeTee."

My aunt replied, "Rebecca Marie is part of our family and she deserves to be treated as such. In fact she belongs with us." All the adults agreed insisting that my daddy bring me more often to visit the family.

I glanced at the adults in conversation feeling as if I was special in this world of happy children. Here, I mattered. When my mother's name came up in conversation all the adults starting talking in another language that I did not understand. It was obvious that no one in this happy house liked Nancy.

What I did not know and I think what my Aunts and Uncles did not know was that this day was a good-bye celebration. The next day my Daddy was going off to sea and might be gone a year or more. My happy world of pretty dresses, sleeping in a warm bed and enjoying hot meals was nearly over. It would be a very long time before I could see this wonderful family again.

That evening my Daddy walked into Nancy's house with me. He handed her an envelope and told her, "This is for TeeTee's Christmas... I am going to Japan and do that route for a year maybe more. I'll send you money every month."

My heart felt like the blood drained out of it as I boldly asked, "Are you going away, Daddy?"

He squatted down and said, "Yes TeeTee

and I'll be gone for a long time. I don't want you to worry. I will be back. I promise."

I panicked and threw my arms around his neck right in front of Nancy and begged him with tears running down my cheeks, "Don't leave me! Take me back to Aunt Louisa... please!"

As always, he said I had to stay. Nancy yanked me out of his arms as I screamed, "Don't leave me!"

He walked out the door without another word as Nancy released me. Her face twisted with fury for what I had just done and said. She ran out after my Daddy where I could hear them shouting in an angry argument. I do not know what they were saying but I did understand what was going to happen to me when Sam chuckled, "You are going to get it now, you stupid idiot."

My head hung down to my chest thinking she was going to kill me this time. When the door flew open, there she stood looking like a demon from hell wearing a lacy apron. The door slammed shut with a crash. I heard Sam giggle in anticipation of the beating I was about to get. However, for once God heard my inner pleas as a knock came to the door. Hester looked out the window and said, "The family is here."

Nancy stared at me with those mean evil green eyes of hers. Then as if a switch someone flicked a switch or the channel changed, Nancy turned happily answering the door with hugs and kisses for the family that had arrived for Thanksgiving Dinner.

This celebration was different from my Daddy's family. Just like at Aunt Louisa's house, there was not enough room at the table for everyone. Therefore, after some short conversation, the adults sat to a feast. I held my MoMo and watched the children, who were not running around in play or happily talking. They all sat like mannequins and watched the television. There was no TV snack and, we all had to watch Wrestling because it was Sam's favorite.

After my sisters cleared dishes from the table, the adults talked and enjoyed desert. Then, Nancy called the children to the table where they ate leftovers; normally I would not have taken notice to this or even cared. I was happy to eat leftover stuffing and mash potatoes but I just could not help making the comparison from my Daddy's family and Nancy's family. Here there were no compliments for the children and all the children seemed to understand they had to be quiet and perfectly behaved. I don't think my cousins were abused, it was just Nancy's family had strict hard rules like my uncle always said, "Children should be seen and not heard."

The cousins did not really talk to me or even acknowledge me now that I think about it. I didn't notice at the time but understood years later that I was an outcast to a certain degree among my mother's family. I was different from everyone else. I did not have blond hair and blue eyes. I was not as tall or as pretty, my hair was not straight and silky. They regarded my Daddy and me as, OUTCASTS, inferiors, stupid and worthless. Nancy's family was very prejudice. They tolerated me because I was not black, my features and color were Hispanic not to say in their eyes that it was accepted but only tolerated. Thereby, they forgave Nancy for her "mistake".

The older children including Ellen and Hester cleared the table and did the dishes while the adults had coffee in the living room. As it grew late, many of the adults who brought children left for home. Only those adults without children stayed and visited with my mother over a game of cards.

Ellen told Hester and me to go to bed. The evening was uneventful and one of peace as I assumed Nancy forgot that she was angry with me.

Early, the next morning Nancy yanked me out of bed causing me to fall to the floor. Startled awake my thoughts were unclear. Nancy was yelling at me and as I pulled myself up the belt came down across my back with a loud clap and a hot surge of pain.

"You want to stay with your Aunt Louisa, huh? You think that nigger bitch is better than I am? I'll teach you who to respect and appreciate," shrieked Nancy.

The belt came at me like a whip across my back, my head, and legs and twice across my left arm like a burning hot branding iron. Over and over again, the belt stung into my flesh. I curled in a ball trying to protect my face. Panting and winded Nancy stopped and stormed out of the room. Hester was on the other bed watching the whole time. I looked up at her and her face was one of complete shock. She said nothing and did nothing; she just looked at me as I began to heave greatly, tears now streamed down my cheeks.

A few minutes passed and Hester still watched me. I stood up, trembling and lost to a crying bout that I could not control. I noticed that I had urinated on the floor and hung my face in shame because Hester now looked at the puddle on the floor. Why didn't Hester help me? Why did she just stare as if I was a freak in a circus?

"You filthy gutter rat! You peed on my nice clean floor," screeched Nancy!

Hester pulled the blanket over her head as a shield. Nancy marched over to me grabbed a hand full of my hair and proceeded to wipe the urine on the floor with my face. Smashing my nose and lips into the hard wood floor and making urine go into my mouth and nose.

Then, she yanked me up by my arm and put me over her knee. She pulled up my nightgown and pulled my panties down. To expose my buttocks was the worst taboo in this house. Then, to make matters worse Sam and Ellen were now standing in the doorway watching. Nancy gave me a hard, fierce spanking with her bare hand. The hot searing pain that went through my buttocks and body was indescribable. She would not stop as I kept glancing up and looking at Sam who was actually laughing!

This crazed spanking had to be hurting Nancy's hand as much as my buttocks was hurting. It seemed like an eternity, she just would not stop until Hester shouted, "Mama... NO!"

Nancy shoved me to the floor and grabbed Hester's face. "Don't you ever tell me what to do or you'll get the same!"

Hester started crying and got back under the covers again. I just lay on the floor like a heap of heaving flesh. Feeling so choked up it was a struggle to cry. Nancy grabbed me by my arm and literally dragged me through the house. She made her way through the kitchen where she opened the door to the garage and tossed me in. The door slammed nearly shaking the whole house.

I lay there for a long while and did not move nearly holding my breath as I felt my body ache and my buttocks throb and burn. Eddie-Boy went up to me, tears in his eyes and held me. When I tried to sit up, I cringed from the pain. I put my hand to my buttocks and felt the skin thick and coarse. I had no panties on and felt so ashamed because Eddie-boy was present. It was a great sin for a girl not to have her panties on.

My nightgown felt sticky and I pulled on the back bringing it forward to see what I sat on. My eyes went wide to see blood. My pretty, new nightgown now stained in blood. I did not really understand why I was bleeding.

Eddie-Boy suggested, "Get some clothes from the laundry..."

Ellen opened the door interrupting Eddie Boy, "Put this on and put that night gown in the wash basin. Boy, you have really done it now. You hurt Mama; she has an ice pack on her hand. You better stay quiet and not pee in your pants again."

I felt astounded, to say the least. Nancy was angry with ME for hurting her! I moved slowly to minimize the pain all over my body, arms, legs and head. I told Eddie-Boy not to watch while I put on panties and flannel pajamas.

I desperately needed to urinate again, but where? I dare not knock on the door for permission to use the toilet. Eddie-boy as always came to my rescue. "I'll go back into the wall so you can pee in private. Climb on the garbage can and pee in the wash basin, be sure to run a little water afterwards," suggested Eddie-Boy

I thanked Eddie-boy and after he disappeared into the wall, I did as he suggested. Then looked at the cold dark corner where my sleeping bag awaited me. It had been a couple of months since I slept on it and now it looked covered in dust. I looked up and could see the spider webs. I hated spiders.

I dressed and then straightened out my sleeping bag and sat on it, keeping an eye on the spiders. I wanted to be ready to jump out of the way if one came at me. I rubbed my buttocks, feeling it hurt and itch something awful. I touched the back of my head and felt a great lump there. The only thought in my mind was, *Please God, Help Me.*

Over that weekend, Nancy drank heavily and several times a day came into the garage and gave me a fierce beating with the belt. Sunday night was the worst, when she swung the belt and let the buckle smash against my face, causing the corner of my eye to bleed and split my upper lip. Even she knew she had gone too far, I could tell by the way she looked at me.

"When you go to school tomorrow, tell your teacher that you fell down the stairs. Do as I say... I warn you," shrieked Nancy!

She nearly flew out of the garage leaving me there trembling in tears holding my lip that would not stop bleeding. A short time later, Hester and Ellen entered the garage.

Ellen said, "Jesus, God! Look what you made her do to you. You better learn to keep your mouth shut or she'll kill you."

Ellen cleaned my wounds while Hester watched, still with that look of shock on her face. When Ellen was done with me, they left the garage. Shortly after, I could hear them talking in the kitchen probably having dinner. No matter, I did not feel like eating anyway. I could hear when they were washing the dinner dishes and waited for Hester or Sam to put out the trash. Hester opened the door slowly and walked down the two steps to the garage floor. She opened the trash and put in a brown paper bag. She walked over to me; I swear she was afraid of me. She looked over her shoulder to be sure no one was watching and she pulled a dinner roll out of her apron pocket and handed it to me. I took it and she ran into the house.

"Hester's not that bad. Go ahead and eat the roll. It's a gift from Hester, she knows if she got caught giving you food she'd get the tar beat out of her," said Eddie-Boy.

I held up the roll and let Eddie-boy take the first bite. I tried to eat it but my lip was raw and spilt and I the inside of my mouth felt cut too. I just could not eat it. I gave it to Eddie-Boy who hid it for later.

At dawn, I woke to excruciating pain. I examined my legs and arms taking notice of the enormous dark black bruises. I could not see my reflection but I felt how terribly swollen my face was. I could taste that metal salty taste of blood in my mouth. My back and head hurt to the point of insanity. My throat felt dry and the thought of a cool drink of water drew me toward the washbasin.

Nancy opened the garage door and looked at me with those angry eyes. "You stupid little fool...

Look at yourself! You are the devil and make me do these things to get me in trouble. You are going to school today and you will tell your teacher if she asks that you fell down the stairs. Tell her that we have a deep basement and you went down the stairs without permission and fell. She will most likely call me and I'll tell her the same thing. If you say something different, you will get me in trouble. You are the bad one, with those devil black eyes of yours."

I looked at her thinking at my tender age that she was a complete nut. Nevertheless, obediently I agreed to tell the teacher that I fell down the basement steps. We had no basement, only two steps from the kitchen door to the garage but I would tell the lie to keep Nancy happy. It was all about survival and I understood completely.

Chapter 5

Keep the Secret

Early the next day, I was called into the bathroom where I got a bath in clean water. My hair shampooed and styled in a ponytail and braid. When I looked at myself in the mirror, my jaw dropped in shock; it looked as if a train hit me. My lip was so swollen and bruised I could not close my mouth. The left side of my face seriously bruised along with a black eye. No amount of grooming would take away from the fact that I was badly beaten. If Nancy had one ounce of common sense she would keep me home until I healed. However, this was not a housc of common sense.

I did not have to walk to the corner to catch the school bus this morning. Nancy drove me to school. I did not say a word but the truth was I was feeling ill. Although I was hungry, I knew I would puke if I ate something. The car stopped in front of the school and Nancy looked at me for a moment before she asked, “What are you going to say, if they ask?”

“I went to the basement without permission and fell down the stairs.”

Nancy nodded, “Good girl. I’ll pick you up after school unless they call me to come and get you early. You know this is your entire fault. You made me hit you. Now, off with you."

I got out of the car and watched it nearly race off for home. I turned and walked up the walkway with my head down, feeling embarrassed for anyone to see me in such a state. Of course, the kids were mean, laughing at me and calling me names. One boy went up to me and laughed, "What the hell happened to you?"

I kept walking feeling near tears. Some kids stared in shock and others whispered to each other or laughed at me. Judy, a girl from my class walked up to me looking concerned. I always saw her at the bus stop and she always had a friendly smile and hello for everyone.

"Rebecca, what happened to you? Are you all right? Maybe you should go to the school nurse," suggested Judy.

I glanced at her and just kept walking without a reply. She stayed by my side telling the other kids to shut up. I got in line in front of my classroom door, which was the rule. Miss Brinks opened the door and rang her little bell. I stood with my head down staring at the back of the shoes of the little boy in front of me. We marched into class one by one. When Miss Brinks saw me, she gasped, "Rebecca... oh my, what happened?"

I do not know what came over me because I loved Miss Brinks so much but I snapped at her, "Nothing happened! Leave me alone!"

She watched me walk to the coat hooks and

hang up my jacket. I tried with all my might to hold back the tears thinking with great regret, *I yelled at Miss Brinks. She is so pretty and so nice. Why am I so bad?*

Miss Brinks remained in the doorway waving her hand to someone. Then, I saw her talking to a man who looked over her shoulder directly at me. I felt so ashamed. Miss Brinks closed the door and went up to me. She put her palm on my forehead and asked me to sit down. I sat on the rug with the rest of the kids who were ALL staring at me as if I had grown a second head. Judy stayed by my side.

A lady walked into the classroom wearing a white dress, white stockings and white shoes with a cute little hat on. Miss Brinks called me over and said, "This is Miss Green, the school nurse. Go with her and I'll be along shortly." I panicked thinking I was in trouble. All I could think to do was to shout, "I'll be good. I'm sorry..."

Miss Green took my hand and calmly said, "Of course you will be good, you are a good girl after all. No need to be afraid, let me put ointment on your lip."

She spoke with such a sweet voice and so I went off with her. In her office, she had me take off all my clothes except, for my panties and undershirt. I was very embarrassed, feeling my face blush red hot. She examined my legs, arms and peeked under my shirt. She pulled the back of my panties to look inside. I flinched knowing it was a terrible sin for her to look at my buttocks. She examined my scalp then took tender care to look at my lip and in fact did put ointment on it. Miss Green took pictures of me from behind and from the front. I was a puppet, making no protest because I just had to do as she said. Miss Green then helped me get dressed.

Miss Green gave me a drink of water and an aspirin that I could chew; it tasted good but stung the inside of my mouth.

Miss Brinks, and a man who identified himself as the school principle, Mr. Wallis walked into the room. They sat and began their questions. At first I did not answer but they were persistent so I went into my rehearsed speech, "I went down into the basement without permission and fell down the stairs."

Miss Green, asked, "Did you fall forward or backward?"

Not prepared for that question I just shrugged my shoulders. Mr. Wallis asked, "Who lives in your home with you?"

Again, I did not expect that question and so I had no answer. Miss Brink asked, "Do you live with your mother and father? Do you have brothers and sisters?"

I stuttered, "My...my father does not live with us. He… he…he's away at sea."

Miss Brink then asked, "Who else lives in your home?"

I replied, “Sam, Hester and Ellen.”

Mr. Wallis then asked, “Are they your brother and sisters?”

I nodded in reply and was surprised when Miss Green just came out and asked, “Who hurt you? Was it your Mother or maybe one of your sisters or... your brother? Someone spanked your bottom terribly, who was it?”

I nearly gasped and firmly stated, “I fell down the stairs!”

Mr. Wallis shook his head as he signed deeply. “Lay down, here in the nurse’s office and rest, Rebecca.”

I liked the feel of the crisp clean sheets and soft pillow. The three of them walked away and whispered to each other. They appeared to be very upset.

Miss Green told me, “Take a nap Rebecca. You will feel a little better after some rest. I’ll be right here.”

Feeling warm and somewhat better, before I knew it, I was asleep. Miss Green woke me up as the bell rang out. It was lunchtime and she brought me a tray with soup, a grill cheese sandwich and a glass of milk. She also had a tray for herself and sat to have lunch with me. Eating was awkward because of my swollen lip and the cuts inside of my cheek making me drool a little.

Miss Green asked me lots of questions about

Nancy and my family. For the most part, I gave no answer. Suddenly, Nancy walked into the room. I immediately looked down to the floor as Nancy put on the performance of a lifetime.

"My poor baby, she had such a nasty fall. I did not want to send her to school but she cried and cried telling me she did not want to miss a day of Miss Brink's class. I just did not have the heart to deny her. She scared me to death when she fell. Will she be all right? Please tell me that my little girl will be all right!"

Nancy then went over and took me in her embrace putting on such a show of love. My god, I think she was even crying. I knew it was a lie. I was only five but she could not fool me.

"Mrs. VanBuren, Rebecca told me she fell down the stairs. You should have taken her to the hospital. I examined her and I believe she will be all right but you should have a doctor check her out. Keep her home for a few days to heal. She has a bit of a fever so I gave her a chewable aspirin." No mention was made about my sore buttocks.

Nancy thanked the nurse a hundred times and assured her that she would take me straight to the doctor. I suppose Miss Green, Miss Brinks, and Mr. Wallis suspected at first that Nancy hand abused me. However, I kept my story straight and after Nancy's performance, all suspicions were gone. I stayed home that entire week, to heal. I never saw a doctor and remained in the cold garage with little food. Nancy did not hit me but threatened me repeatedly and called me terrible names making me feel frightened.

When she thought, she had the people at school convinced that I was just a clumsy fool, the beatings returned and the starvation continued at home. Most of the time, I didn't have a sack lunch or money to buy lunch but Miss Green or Miss Brinks always saw to it that I had a hot lunch. They were so nice to me. Despite how the kids made fun of me and picked on me, I always look forward to going to school. To Miss Brinks and Miss Green I was a person who mattered.

Nancy's theatrics became something to marvel at, she was good at fooling people despite my appearance. Moreover, I always lied to protect her. Strangely, I did not hate Nancy. Yes, I was afraid of her but I still loved her and all I really wanted was for her to love me, to show me that she was proud to have me as her daughter. I always believed that one day she would accept me and there would be peace between us.

From Thanksgiving weekend to Christmas, I missed many days of school. I kept getting sick and Miss Green firmly stated that I was not to go to school if I had a fever. I guess my Daddy sent Nancy plenty of money to pay the bills because she never went to work and was always home for the most part. Although, many weekends she would come home very late into the night or spend a day or two away but, she was home in time for church on Sunday. She never missed church. Hester, Ellen and I went to church every Sunday unless I was sick or had bruises on my face.

Christmas, to say the least was bewildering for me. I remembered my father gave her an envelope and said "This is for TeeTee's Christmas" I suppose money was in the envelope but all I received for Christmas that year was the great privilege of being allowed Christmas dinner and at this point in time, all I wanted or cared about was dinner. I was indeed starving and food was all that was important to me. I really did not care about toys all I wanted was a heavy blanket and hot food.

Nancy was in a good mood that Christmas. She allowed me to watch It's a Wonderful life on TV, followed by the best dinner of my life. I got new warm pajamas and slept in the house. Eddie-boy was always by my side. I always held up the first spoon full so he could have the first bite. We both slept in a warm clean bed and felt life could not be better. However, I ruined everything with my clumsiness. This time it was my fault.

Hester called out, "Rebecca Marie! Bugs Bunny is on ... come and watch it with me."

Well, in my excitement I ran into the living room and bumped a table whereupon, I knocked down the silver framed picture of Nancy's children causing the glass to break. Hester turned wide-eyed and ran to the safety of her bedroom. I stood there frozen, terrified at what I had just done.

Nancy stormed into the room and looked at me then to the broken picture on the floor. She slapped me with all her might, knocking me to the floor. I think she was yelling at me, but I don't really remember. I saw her pick up the frame as if it were a precious treasure worth great sums of money. She grabbed me by the back of my collar and put me over her knee. Sam was now in the room watching as always. She pulled my pajama bottoms and panties down and proceeded to give me a severe spanking.

Sam was laughing and I was beyond humiliation. He watched me get a horrible spanking and could see my naked buttocks, and of course, to bare my buttocks was the most horrible sin in the world.

Nancy shoved me off her lap; I am not sure if she stopped because she was tired or because her hand hurt as much as my buttocks did. She screamed, "Get in that garage right now. How dare you break the picture of my children... get out of my sight before I kill you!"

I ran into the garage and back to my dirty sleeping bag. Eddie-boy came up to me as I released a stream of tears. My behind was sore, burning and itching to the point of madness.

"Eddie-Boy, I broke the picture of her children. Why am I so stupid? I ruined everything!"

Eddie-boy comforted me while I got my

wits about me, and then Nancy entered the garage for a session of punishment. I was in serious trouble, it was still Christmas Vacation and so she did not have to worry about anyone seeing me for a few days. Thereby, she let loose, hitting me this way and that way, my body flying from one side of the garage to the other. It was as if I were a rag doll. I did not realize it but I was screaming for help. Our next-door neighbor could hear me and called the police.

This was not the first time the police came to our house. Quite often, when Nancy was not home Ellen and Hester would play their music loud while their friends were visiting. There was talk that they were smoking and drinking beer. However, this was the first time the police came to the house because of me.

Sam ran into the garage and gasped, “It’s the cops! I think nosy Mrs. Pena called them.”

My mother heard pounding at the door and a burly man’s voice shout, “Open up, this is the police!” She ran her fingers through her hair and took a deep breath before she hurried off to open the door.

Sam looked at me with a hateful glare and spat, “You are always causing trouble... pig!”

I sat sobbing and trembling not really understanding all that was happening. Whatever happened, no one came to my rescue. To this day I have no idea how Nancy was always able to calm any situation even with the police. No doubt, Nancy gave a spectacular performance of lies.

It was daybreak before Nancy came back in the garage to deal with me. She was serious in her manner, speaking with low even tones. "Do you want to go to prison? Do you know that in prison you have to take a shower naked in front of everyone and even use the toilet while everyone watches? The people there will take turns beating you up... everyday... is that what you want?"

I shook my head in fear wondering where this was leading too. "If you ever talk to the police or anyone about what happens here in this garage, or in this house you will go to prison and stay there till the day you die. Remember that!"

Nancy left me alone in the garage to think about what she told me. I swore to Eddie-boy that we would never tell a living soul what happens in the garage or in Nancy's house. I certainly did not want to go to prison.

Chapter 6

Torment

January second, I returned to school afraid to speak to anyone. I had to keep the family secrets. For the most part, my beatings amounted to only the routine smack upside my head and the never-ending scolding. Like the time Nancy entered the bathroom and I had not put on my panties yet. She ranted and raved, preaching the evil of exposing the private parts of the body. She forced me to kneel and pray with her in hopes god would forgive me my indecency.

Nancy mainly punished me by denying me food to such an extent I always felt sick and exhausted making it difficult to stay awake. I did get a meal at school, Miss Brinks and Miss Green always saw to it. They always questioned me about Nancy but I kept the secret fearing prison.

Weekends were the hardest for me. I would go from Friday afternoon until Lunch at School on Monday with no food at all. Then, I would eat my lunch to the last crumb and end up with a stomachache. I just could not win.

Easter vacation came and spring was in the air. Hunger is all that dominated my thoughts. I sat in the garage hoping and praying for food when

Hester came into the garage to put the evening's trash out. She always looked at me with such fear in her eyes; I guess I looked ghastly. Nancy said I always had the look of the devil in my eyes. After Hester went back into the house without saying a word to me, I just stared at the garbage can. I had to eat... anything.

Eddie-boy walked with me to the silver can and we opened the lid. I knew this was wrong but I was so darn hungry. We dug through the can and found the table scrapes. I dug my fingers in and ate up as much as I could. I do not remember what it tasted like; good or bad, but it was food and anything was better than having nothing.

Eating out of the trash became a regular routine until Sam caught me. Of course, he ran to Nancy, "I saw Rebecca Marie eating trash ... Like a pig!"

Nancy walked into the garage with Sam and just looked at me. "Oh, so you want to be a pig now? Sam put the trash outside. I do not want the trash in the garage anymore. Rebecca Marie, I will teach you to act like a pig. Get on that floor and crawl around... in a circle and do not stop until I tell you too."

I made the mistake of hesitating because even at my age her request of me was so humiliating. She smacked me hard and knocked me to the floor. Sam returned from putting the trash out and began laughing at me as I crawled around,

"Make her say Oink, Oink!" Laugh Sam.

Nancy laughed and commanded me to Oink like a pig and not to stop until she told me too. There I was, crawling around in a circle oinking like a pig. Tears choked me and I stuttered "O...on...oink." She grabbed a piece of clothesline and repeatedly whipped my buttocks shouting at me to oink louder and quicker. My god, can it get worst than this?

After a long while, I guess both Nancy and Sam got bored with this ridiculous display. Nancy then ordered, "Get up, and stop acting like an animal. You will eat when I say so and not before."

That is when I noticed that Ellen and Hester were standing in the doorway watching me. I looked at Hester knowing she was terrified of Nancy. At least she was lucky and never beaten, only threatened on occasion.

My return to school was a short-lived relief. The kids were mean to me. The boys would make me trip and fall and then mimic my stuttering saying, "Re... Re... be... be... ca... Ma... Ma... Reee" The girls would make fun of my appearance, my clothes and call me ugly Olive Oil because I was so skinny. My head always hurt and sleep was so hard to fight when I was at school. I just wanted peace and quiet but found none in school. School only meant food to me and the rest of the time, I just wanted escape.

One night, I got a fierce spanking, but this

time Nancy's joy was to humiliate me. She went on and on about how sinful and evil it was for girls to show their private parts. "Only very bad girls would allow their body to be naked in front of anybody." She made sure that Hester, Ellen and Sam were agreeing with her. I stood there with my head dropped to my chest praying this madness would end.

To my horror, Nancy ordered, "Strip!" I looked up and she repeated, "Take off all your clothes, NOW! Don't make me say it again."

I took off all my clothes except my panties and undershirt. I glanced at Ellen and Sam who were giggling. Then, Nancy ordered, "I said everything!"

I started to cry. I could not take off everything in front of everyone and god. But, before I knew it, my body crashed to floor from the smack that Nancy gave me. She glared at me as I stood up and hung my head in shame. I dropped my panties and removed my undershirt. There I stood naked!

Nancy then said, "Look at you, you are disgusting... you are so bony and ugly... Jesus God, I can see your privates! You make me sick." Tears began running down my cheeks as Nancy continued, "You are to stand there without moving. If you move, you will get a good spanking."

I stood in the middle of the living room, naked, my dignity stripped from me. Tears rolled down my cheeks but I said nothing and did nothing.

I stood there until my legs and back hurt. I stood for so long that I started to lose my balance a few times. Sam made faces at me and tossed crumpled up newspaper at me being sure to hit me on my buttocks or my pelvis area. Eddie-boy was not present; he knew never to be present if I was naked. My head hurt, I was hungry and beyond exhaustion. I don't know how long I stood there, but it was more than I could bear when Nancy shouted at me. "Put your clothes on and get in the garage!" which I immediately did.

Once in the garage Nancy told me, "Pray to God to forgive you for standing naked with no shame. If he forgives you then I will too."

The door slammed and I simply wept. It was not my idea to stand naked in front of everyone. I sat on my sleeping bag where Eddie-boy awaited me. Many hours passed without a word between us, it grew dark and cold as my stomach growled. I watched the door hoping and praying for food, but I could see from under the door when the light went out. Once the light was out, that meant Kitchen closed.

I cried so hard I felt my body shake. When I grew tired of crying, I sat quite for a moment then heard a click. The door opened a little and Hester put something on the step and quietly closed the door. I waited for a moment then went over to the steps. There was a paper napkin with three cookies on it. I smiled thinking they were heavenly. I whispered, “Thank you, Hester. Thank you, god.”

The next day, I went to school feeling worn-out. I was always in pain so much so that at times I could not tell where the pain was coming from. The day was a normal routine, uneventful but I did get a hot lunch that was beyond delicious.

As I walked from the bus stop toward the house, Mrs. Pena went up to me, looking from side to side checking to see if anyone was watching. She grabbed my hand and asked, “Rebecca, are you all right? Does she hurt you? Tell me sweetheart. You can trust me... I can help you. I’ll call the police.”

Well, at the mention of police I sternly stated without a stutter, “My Mama doesn’t hurt me; she loves me and gives me mash potatoes all the time.” With that, I ran for home terrified that I might go to prison. After that day, Mrs. Pena always offered me something to eat but I never took her food and would always run away from her. I wish I could see her today and thank her for wanting to help me.

Summer finally arrived and that meant that Nancy started staying away from home again. I was always curious as to where she went or what she did. Ellen was in charge again and that was Okay with me but now Sam took power into his hands. He finished school and had a job but when he came home, he took it upon himself to torment me as his entertainment.

Ellen always reinforced the importance of

never taking my panties off when I took a bath. She would always leave the bathroom when I changed into clean panties because she really believed it was sinful to expose my rear end. Sam listened to these lectures and used what he heard as a way to make my life even tougher.

I usually wore play-clothes, which consisted of a pair of pants made with an elastic waist and a blouse. Sam sat on the porch and watched me riding my bike, one of the biggest pleasures I had during the summer. Sam then called over a group of boys playing ball. I saw him talking to them then he tossed the ball toward me.

"Rebecca Marie, bring the ball here," asked Sam with a sly smile.

Always eager to please I got off my bike picked up the ball and ran over to him whereupon, I handed him the ball. I turned to walk back to my bike when suddenly I felt Sam yank on my pants pulling them down along with my panties in front of all the boys who immediately laughed. They laughed so hard some were bending over and clapping their thighs.

I was shocked beyond words... the humiliation took me by surprise as I quickly pulled my pants up and ran toward the house. The front door was locked because I was not allowed in the house until Ellen called me in. She would not open the door no matter how much I pounded.

Sam called out, "I'm sorry... I didn't mean

it. Come get your bike."

I was crying as I turned and took notice that all the boys had stopped laughing and seemed genuinely sorry. I walked over to get my bike having to pass by them. When, one of the boys, I don't know which one YANKED my pants down exposing my rear end again. They laughed as more kids gathered to laugh at me. I was beyond humiliation and ran over to the side gate to find a place to hide from them all. The gate was locked! They were laughing and calling me 'Butt Girl" Tears streamed from my eyes when Ellen finally opened the door, "What the hell is happening out here?"

I turned and ran behind Ellen choking on my tears and looking for escape, for a place to hide. Sam could hardly contain himself as he laughed thunderously.

Hester said, "I saw from the window, Sam and the other boy pulled Rebecca Marie's pants down."

Ellen scolded, "You are a sick bastard. Leave her alone ... don't you have something better to do?"

After slamming the door Ellen told me to go watch TV with Hester and to stop making such a fuss. How could she think I was overreacting when she was always telling me how sinful it was for people to see my buttocks. I sat sobbing in front of the TV unable to enjoy it. I just wanted to die.

Within a few days, throughout the neighborhood the children nicknamed me 'Butt Girl". All the boys would try to pull my pants down. I became so afraid I no longer went out to ride my bike when I had the chance. I spent time in the garage by choice or in the backyard with Eddie-Boy. Sam called me names and told such terrible things about my body being ugly and nobody wanted to see it anyway. He said I was a freak and only good to laugh at.

One Saturday, Ellen invited her friends over to play records. She ordered me to stay in the bedroom. It was in the evening and dark out. I could smell pizza, which made my mouth water. I turned off the light and quietly opened the bedroom door a tiny bit to observe what was going on.

The living room was nearly pitch-black save for the lit cigarettes. I could make out that a few couples were sitting in chairs and on the couch kissing. I just had to have some pizza. I crawled out into the hallway thinking because it was so dark I could make it through the living room without anyone noticing. My plan was to grab a slice of pizza, back to the bedroom and eat it.

My attempt was foolish. Of all the people in the room, of course I bumped into Sam. He picked me up by the scruff of my neck and marched to the bedroom where he tossed me on the bed. Ellen was right behind him and angrily scolded me for leaving the bedroom. Sam whispered to her then she ordered me to the bathroom. I ran into the bathroom where Ellen told me to use the toilet so I would not have an excuse to get up again.

When I returned to the bedroom, Ellen warned, as she pointed at the chair in the corner covered in coats and sweaters. "If you get out of bed again, the clothes-monster will get you and toss you into hell! I am not kidding, so don't try it."

Ellen turned the light off and closed the door. The room was dark with only a tiny ray of light coming through the window. I stared at the chair in the corner thinking it did in fact, look like a monster, in the dark room. I found it strange that no one ever spoke of a clothes-monster before.

The smell of pizza and other foods became irresistible. I decided to peek again to see what was happening in the living room in hopes of something to eat. I sat up and put both feet on the floor keeping my eyes on the chair, in the corner. I stood up and took a couple of steps toward the door. From the corner, a dark large figure stood up with a growl and came at me.

I cannot remember if I screamed or tried to run, maybe I stood frozen. The next thing I knew the clothes-monster picked me up to toss me into hell. Instead, I hit the wall with the back of my head, hard! Ellen ran into the room and turned the light on. I do not remember all that happened, I was dazed and I think I could hear myself moan. Either there seemed to be lots of movement in the room, by people or maybe the room was moving. I had the feeling of falling in slow motion. When I felt like I finally fell on the bed, even though I already was on the bed, things suddenly became clear.

I could hear Ellen yelling about the dent on the wall. She picked me up and put me back into my own bed and shouted, "Next time the clothes-monster will send you to hell... where you belong. Now, stay in bed!"

Needless to say, I did not get out of bed. I rubbed the bump on the back of my head and kept my eye on the chair in the corner, fearing the clothes-monster. I found out years later that it was Sam posing as a clothes-monster. I think he only meant to scare me. Nevertheless, I was hurt and the next day Nancy was in a rage wanting to know what happened to cause the dent on the wall. To her, the dent always remained a mystery.

At times, I felt completely drained. Drawing my picture journals was my only way to hold onto some degree of sanity. My pictures grew more brutal as time passed. I drew pictures of killing Sam and cutting him apart. In addition, I drew pictures of the mean neighborhood kids in prison, cut and bleeding. Anger filled my heart as I wondered about my Daddy. Why didn't he care about me? He told me that he loved me.

Chapter 7

Humiliation

It was August again and Nancy anxiously groomed me from head to toe. My Daddy arrived with a great smile on his face. I however had no smile to offer him. I was void of emotion, heartless and unhappy. He embraced me but I stood like a mannequin despite it felt so wonderful to be in his arms.

"What's the matter TeeTee, aren't you happy to see me? I missed you very much."

I had no reply and just walked around to the passenger side of the car waiting to get in. We drove off without a word then he parked the car and turned to talk to me.

"Are you all right, why the long face?"

I simply replied, "Can I stay with you? Can I come and live with you?"

He signed in frustration, "TeeTee, I can't take care of a little girl. My ship leaves for sea in a few weeks. I just don't have the place or the time."

Tears welled in my eyes because I came to realize it was true he did not want me... just like Nancy said.

Eddie-boy whispered in my ear. "Don't ruin it, he'll take you to eat and you can at least spend a little time away from home." I nodded as we drove off.

We went to the Chinese Restaurant and then to the lake to feed the ducks. I have to admit I loved going to the restaurant and had so much fun feeding the ducks. Over the next few weeks, my father visited every Sunday and bought me a new wardrobe for school. Then, just like before, that last day he drove me back home I let lose, crying and pleading for him not to leave me. Just like all the times before, it was for nothing as I watched him drive off.

I was in the first grade now and I did not see Miss Brinks anymore. My new teacher was older and rather mean. Miss Green was happy to see me and so was Mr. Wallis. The kids however, could not be meaner to me. Calling me names, pushing me, and treating me as if I was an intrusion in their happy lives. It just seemed that everyone hated me for just being me.

Now my daydreams turned to plotting how I could run away to a better happier place, it's all I ever thought about. Once my father left, my life returned to beatings, hunger and humiliation. Nancy forced me to pray for my sins and at times, she would beat me in the name of God. Why did God hate me so much?

At school, the little boy who sat behind me thought it would be funny to put gum in my hair. I was completely unaware of it. I wore my hair in a ponytail and did not feel him put a wad of bubble gum in my hair. All day the kids kept giggling and pointing at me and I had no idea why. When I got home, I had to change my clothes into play-clothes, a typical habit, just about every child in my neighborhood changed into play-clothes after school. When I came out of the bathroom, I waited for Nancy's command.

Ellen asked, "What is that in your hair?"

Nancy examined my ponytail then grabbed hold of it. She angrily dragged me to the garage by my hair where she proceeded to yank out the gum, cursing and yelling the whole time.

"What the hell is this? Just how and when did you get gum?" Spat Nancy.

I protested explaining I did not have gum and I did not know anything about how it got into my hair. Well, all hell broke loose. Nancy shouted, "How dare you lie to me!"

She repeatedly smacked me, making my head uncontrollably go from left to right until I hit the floor. Nancy put me over her knee and spanked me brutally until my buttocks felt like it was on fire. She stood panting and left me to myself. Then she returned with a stick in her hand. "I'll show you to lie to me."

Most of the beating is a blur in my memory. It felt like she whipped me within an inch of my life. I could hear the loud clap of the cane against my flesh. She hit me so much my clothes began to tear. I tried to get away but found the door locked. I was now afraid for my life as she struck me with an object. I cannot remember what that object was but suddenly my head hit the washbasin. Everything went quiet then faded to black.

I was beat so badly Nancy kept me home from school. As I look back, I think Nancy was afraid of what she did to me. I had no idea what I looked like but she kept opening the kitchen door just to look at me without a word spoken.

Nancy denied me any food and I felt all the strength drained from my body. I wet my pants a few times unable to move from the pain. I began sleeping nearly around the clock. I held onto my MoMo and Eddie-boy praying to God for help but no help came and no food came.

I do not know how many days I was kept in that state. Nancy took a washcloth to my face and had me dress in school clothes. She drilled me about what I was to tell the people at school if they asked but my mind was in a haze.

Once at school I had little memory about the day's events. I do remember sitting at my desk and hearing the kids whisper and giggle. I remember Miss Nellie addressing me but for some reason I could not hear her. Miss Nellie walked toward me, but my mind went blank and I just cannot remember what happened.

The next thing I knew I was in Miss Green's office lying on the bed. She put a cold, wet towel to my head and I think she was asking me questions but I cannot remember a word spoken between us if any at all.

Before I knew it, Mr. Wallis was telling me with a frantic tone, “You’ll be all right. Don’t worry sweetie!”

Suddenly, I felt the bed rolling down the hallway as Mr. Wallis and Miss Green ran alongside me. Was I dreaming ... what was happening? The next thing that comes to mind I am in a room with upside down bottles hanging over my bed, tubes are hanging down and I can feel my head wrapped in something. A lady dressed just like Miss Green told me, “Hello sweetheart, you are safe in the hospital.”

I had no reply wondering how I got to a hospital. Then, a lady identified herself as Mrs. Castora, “Sweetie, don’t worry you are safe now. Can you tell me what happened to you?”

I turned my head and saw Miss Green there too but she did not have her white uniform on, she wore a black skirt and pink blouse. She gave a big envelope to Mrs. Castora and said, “These are the pictures I took. You have to get her out of that environment before it is too late.”

Miss Green turned to me, “Don’t worry Rebecca, we’ll help you. But you must tell us who hurt you... how did this happen to you?”

To be honest, most of what was said that day I do not remember but I am pretty sure I kept the secret. I loved being in the hospital. There were lots of little girls in the room with me, each in their own bed. From what I remember, Nancy never came to visit me. The nurses were so nice, always bathing me, feeding me and talking so sweet. I slept a lot and finally got the bandage off my head. I guess I had a serious injury on the left side of my head from hitting it on the washbasin.

Then the happy day came and Miss Castora entered with my MoMo and handed it to me. "I thought you might want this," she said.

She had a little suitcase with writing on it. I could not read therefore I didn't know what it said. Miss Castora explained that she went to my house and brought me some clothes. I was discharge from the hospital where I said good-bye to all the nurses that I like to think were angels who took care of me. Once in Miss Castora's car she told me, "You are not going back to your mother. I am taking you to a new home where you'll be safe and happy."

For some strange reason I panicked wondering why this was happening. Where was Nancy? I said nothing but felt my heart hammer in fear as we drove off.

Mrs. Castora took me to the most beautiful happy home in the world. There were other little girls there too. I stayed there for a wonderful week. The little girls in this house did not tease me and were happy to have me there. The couple who ran the foster-house was perfect and loving. I wanted to stay there forever but my court day arrived and off I went with Mrs. Castora.

Once in court I sat with my MoMo in hand and waited to see what this place was about. Nancy walked in with a man wearing a suit. The Judge hit his little hammer on his desk and the hearing began. I did not understand what the adults were saying until... Nancy took the stage.

"I love my little girl! I would never hurt her. She keeps falling down, what can I do about it?" wept Nancy.

Mrs. Castora stood up and began an argument insisting that I stay in the home of the Crugers. This went on for a long time when finally the Judge hit his hammer on his desk again. I did not know what happened but I noticed tears in Mrs. Castora's eyes. She went up to me and hugged me saying, "I am so sorry, sweetheart. I tried, I really tried."

Nancy took my hand and glared at Miss Castora. I was yanked away back to hell. I did not fight or resist. I just went along thinking God had abandoned me again. I must have done something to upset the Crugers and so I did not deserve to live in their home.

Nancy was on probation and the court ordered that Mrs. Castora monitor my home situation. At first, she came once a week and then a couple of times a month. Mrs. Castora would stop by to talk to Nancy and check on me. I did not understand the details at the time but I did understand that Nancy was furious with the whole situation.

I of course was well rehearsed in how to reply to Mrs. Castora's every question. Nancy gave a top performance at every visit having to show proof that she attended her parenting class.

However, right after Miss Castora's visit, my hell returned. My punishment changed somewhat. I did not get beat any more because Nancy would be in a lot of trouble if Miss Castora found a mark on my body. Now, humiliation and a test of endurance was my punishment. Making me crawl like a pig, standing in ice-cold water or, standing on one spot with my arms out to a side for long periods and the worst was when she made me get naked. On those days, it unsettled me to feel so vulnerable in front of God.

One day after Mrs. Castora left, Nancy went into a rage. I could tell she wanted to beat me to death but she could not lay hand on me. Moreover, she was infuriated that she had to be sure I ate three meals a day. On this particular day, she looked at me with her evil glare and ordered me to strip down. Tears came to my eyes as I stepped back in protest whereupon, Nancy screeched, "Take off your clothes!" With that Ellen, Hester and Sam entered the room to watch. I slowly took off my clothes and stared at the floor. Then, to my horror Sam said, "Do the pig thing."

Nancy then ordered, "Get on your hands and knees and oink like a pig."

Like a fool, I ran to the door for escape but Sam hurried and blocked me. Trapped, my protest only made Nancy angrier as she sat down for a long session of torment. Yes, I went down on all fours and crawled around crying and oinking like a pig, completely naked.

She made me spread my butt-cheeks for everyone to see my anus. She called me terrible names, most of the words I had no comprehension of at the time; I just knew they were bad. This went on for what seemed to be hours. Ellen and Hester left the room and together Sam and Nancy had their fun. Nancy made me put my head down to the floor with my buttocks up in the air and she made me say, "That's for you God... I am a pig and a slut. Kiss my ass."

Well, I knew God would never come to my rescue now. I certainly insulted him and angered him. Ellen called out that dinner was ready and I was forced to eat my dinner naked as Nancy said, "You evil thing! You have no shame sitting there naked in front of us. You'll surely burn in hell."

What hurt the most was when she grabbed my MoMo out of my hands and pushed his face into the radiator in the living room and caused a deep black burn across his cheek and one eye. She tossed him at me and said, "That should be you!"

I grabbed my MoMo, held him to my heart,

and blew on his face to sooth the burn. She hurt my MoMo and nothing could be worse than that.

I endured this mental abuse for months until Nancy's probation was over. At this point, I preferred the beatings to the humiliation. She conditioned me to believe my body was a disgrace, a deformity that offended God. She conditioned me to believe I was a worthless parasite placed in Nancy's world... a place I did not belong.

That summer Nancy stayed home, the whole summer. Now, unable to go to school or face anyone outside of the house my life in the garage became a living nightmare, a combination of humiliation and physical abuse. I returned to praying to God for forgiveness but I received no reply.

As usual, my father returned in time to buy me school clothes and spend a few Sundays with me. I must have looked like Hell because on two occasions, my father and Nancy argued terribly and I could hear my name continually come up.

Nevertheless, he did nothing to help me and went away again. I was in second grade now and once again, Mrs. Castora came to my rescue. My teacher called the police because how badly bruised and that appeared confused. Mrs. Castora removed me from Nancy's home for two days but in the end, the Judge sent me back home to her and my living hell. MoMo and Eddie-boy were my only source of salvation.

Chapter 8

Biscuits and Gravy

Most people feel that cemeteries are rather depressing. They can be to the average person because cemeteries have a sense of finality; death always connects to loss and heartbreak. However, I am not the average person. Cemeteries hold just the opposite for me. They are a place of wonderment, history and filled with love by what I read on tombstones. I like cemeteries. My second best thing to enjoy is ... biscuits and gravy. What is the connection with cemeteries and biscuits and gravy, is no doubt your first thought?

Most of my life I occasionally stop and admire a cemetery, especially an old cemetery. I like to read the tombstones and to admire the polished grounds. The great green trees that offer such peaceful shade, the thick green foliage and the simple tranquility of quite save for a bird song or two. There is so much more in this world than the obvious.

I was now eight years old and became a recluse, no friends, no one to talk to, just me Eddie-boy and MoMo. I had not eaten for days. Summer was the worst for me now that Nancy was always home. Ellen graduated from High School and got a full time job, thereby Nancy brought her boyfriend's home. Hester was out of control, after boys and therefore undependable.

On this special day, I felt light-headed and I was filthy to boot. Nancy only allowed me to bathe once or twice a month. My hair was very long, so long in fact that I could sit on it. Having that much hair and never washing it, well, you can imagine how I felt and looked.

Ellen combed my hair into a ponytail and then braided it as an illusion of looking clean. Always being so dirty as a child made me feel filthy as I grew into an adult. I could never seem to take enough baths to get the imaginary filth off me but, I digress ...

Anyway, I was a mess and my father was away at sea, as usual. Feeling alone, I got this idea to run away from home. I thought I could get a job cleaning houses and live in people's garages. I was only eight years old; therefore, I did not understand how impossible that would be. It was Saturday and that meant Nancy was not home, she was never home on weekends since Ellen had weekends off. Nancy, the holier-than-thou church lady was with one of her many boyfriends, no doubt.

However, this was good, Ellen was in charge when Nancy was not home and she Ellen did not give a damn where I was, so long as I was not within her sight. Early in the morning, I set out on my new life of independence. I walk to Brownstone

Road and then to the town park which had an indoor public pool, a super large playground and a nature trail. Back in those days, the park looked beautiful during the summertime. In general, my town was a simple place in the early 60's, mostly apricot orchards.

At the park, I sat and watched the children at play while their parents set up picnic tables. I was so hungry that I just could not watch them set the coals and start cooking up the burgers and hot dogs. I walked down to the creek and followed the path until it ended. Back then, there was a really, old section of the cemetery at the end of the trail. It was rundown and abandoned. In fact, I did not even notice it was a cemetery. I just thought it was neat that the grass was nearly as tall as me. I ran into the grass in play momentarily forgetting my troubles.

Suddenly, I noticed a crooked cross, the wood dry and splintered. I started looking around and found many crosses buried in the tall grass. Then, I found a bench all rotten and worn; it was in a circle shape around a tree trunk. I sat there looking at one particular cross. I wondered why the crosses were nearly hidden and forgotten in this place.

An old man came up to me and asked me what I was doing there all alone. I replied that I was just resting. He sat next to me and told me as he offered his hand, “They call me Grady, how about you?”

I replied, "I am Rebecca Marie at home but at school everyone calls me Rebecca."

Grady asked, "What does your father call you?"

I told him that my father always called me TeeTee and that I did not know why he called me that.

Grady nodded, "Every papa has a special name for the apple of his eye."

Grady took my hand and said, "You ran away from home, didn't you? You can't run away, not from your family and not your situation. Not yet, anyway. Tell me all about what troubles you."

I hung my head and mumbled that nothing was wrong and I had not run away. I told him, "I am just resting. I am here with my family on a picnic. My Dad is making burgers on the grill and so I better get back."

Grady turned to his side and picked up a little bucket, like the kind people buy those candles in to rid a patio of mosquitoes. It had a lid on it like an old fashion jar and he said as he pulled out a piece of bread and handed it to me, "Can't lie to me. Your family didn't come on a picnic. You are alone and have run away. You are safe here and can confide in me. Eat the bread. I have some gravy here to dip it in and some lemon grass tea to wash it down."

I told him, "That's Okay, I'm not hungry."

Grady kind of chuckled and pushed the bread at me. He opened the jar of gravy and dipped his bread, as he said, "I know hungry when I see it. Eat up."

Well, he seemed so nice and even though the gravy looked disgusting to me, I dipped the bread and took a bite. It was delicious! I began eating, suddenly he pulled the bread from me and scolded in a fatherly way of concern, "Eat real slow, you haven't eaten in a good while, if you eat too fast you'll get a belly ache."

I thought it strange that he knew I had not eaten, but I dismissed it. I was so hungry and as I ate slowly, I gobbled down the bread and gravy. Then, he insisted that I drink the lemon grass tea explaining it will help me not to get a bellyache.

All the while, as we ate, he told me about himself. He said that he foolishly wasted his life. He said he left his family in Virginia to make his fortune in California. He told me he lost everything and never saw his family again.

I felt so good to eat that I warmed up to this wonderful soul who fed me. I asked Grady what he was doing here in the cemetery. He told me, "I'm the grounds keeper."

Well, even as a child, I could see that Grady had not cleaned the grounds in a very long time, maybe years. He went on to explain, "I'm too old now and this grass grows so fast. I need clippers to trim it down. I can't even see the markers anymore."

I asked, "Are the crosses, markers?"

Grady replied, "Yeah, the crosses represent the whole of a man's life. There is more bodies buried here than crosses that stand. Some lives were not even worth a cross. One day I'll get clippers and trim down the grounds and give these poor souls some degree of respect."

I told Grady, "There are clippers in my garage at home."

Grady smiled, his face so wrinkled that his eyes nearly got lost in all the deep cracks.

Grady replied, "Thank you. If you can bring the clippers next time, I would appreciate it." Well, I made him happy and that made me feel simply wonderful.

"You can beat Nancy; you have a light within you that she fears. But you need to learn how to take care of yourself first," said Grady, with such a look of purpose, such a look that made me feel like he could actually see into my heart and soul.

Grady picked out of the tall grass three empty quart bottles of Coke Cola and explained, "Take these bottles to the market. Give them to the cashier and tell them you want to sell them. They'll give you 25 cents for each bottle. Then, go to the bakery and ask the lady there for a bag of broken cookies. She'll give you lots for a quarter. Then, hide them in your garage, eat a little bit at a time to the last crumb. You'll have 50 cents left so use each quarter to buy broken cookies as you run out. When you feel really tired and hungry and can't bear it, go through the neighbor's trash and dig up Coke, Pepsi or any kind of glass pop bottles and they'll buy them from you at the store. Go to that little store they call Penny Wise and buy the penny candy. Now this food is junk but it will keep you going. If you sell enough bottles then buy cans of beans and bury them in the back yard so Nancy won't find them.

When you are hungry sneak a can-opener, go to the orchard, and eat the beans. Go ahead and take the apricots from the trees but don't eat too many at a time or you'll get sick."

Then Grady instructed me, "Go to Pete's fill-in station and go into the bathroom to wash your face, behind your ears. You can do that as often as you like, they never have a locked door like other fill-in stations. Bring me those clippers next Saturday and I'll meet you right here."

Grady kissed the back of my hand and I thanked him and promised to return. I picked up the bottles, went to the store and sold them. Then, I went into the bakery. Back in those days' bakeries, butcher shops and such were commonplace, not like today with giant super markets that house everything you'll ever need under one roof. I shyly entered the bakery and told the lady behind the counter, "I want 25 cents worth of broken cookies, please."

She opened up a white paper bag and started shoveling in broken cookies. I was wide-eyed to see she was giving me so much. She handed me the bag and took my quarter then she said, in a funny accent, I think she was Italian, "What's your name?" I told her "My family calls me Rebecca Marie but at school I am called Rebecca." For some insane reason I had the need to explain that to everyone.

She gave me a small single serving of chocolate milk and asked me which my favorite cookie was. I told her I liked the black and white because I like the swirl. She smiled and said, "I'll save the broken black and white cookies for you."

Well, I was so happy! I got Chocolate Milk! Now the trick was to get home and hide these treasures and not get caught. It was late in the afternoon by now and everyone would be home. Therefore, I hid my delicious cookies and delightful chocolate milk in the orchard behind our house. BIG MISTAKE.

When I had the opportunity to get back to the orchard the bag was swarming in ants. The milk seemed Okay but my cookies had ants all over them. Well... waste not, want not. I took each piece and cleaned them off shaking the ants off and leaving them the crumbs. I gathered my goodies and hid them in the garage. That night, I was being punishment for some unknown reason to me and as usual, I had to sleep in the garage. I sat on my sleeping bag on the garage floor. That night as the moon shown through the small window and lit where I sat to enjoy my feast, I shared cookies and Chocolate milk with Eddie-Boy. I kept looking at the two quarters I had left and smiled with such delight. Over the next week, I went to the bakery and bought more cookies and the bakery lady always gave me chocolate milk to wash them down, free of charge!

Oh Saturday, I woke early and stole away the hedge clippers and ran off to visit Grady. When I got there, he was waiting with his gravy and biscuits. I found out that is all he ate because he had no teeth. I told him I did just as he said and how the bakery lady gave me Chocolate milk Free of charge. He began to tell me how I could survive on junk food but that when I had the opportunity to get real food, to stock up.

I always carried a little purse and so, Grady advised, "When food is available eat a little and put a little in your purse for later. But don't let anyone notice."

Grady admired the clippers and said, "I want you to help me with this grave first. I want the area around it as clean as a whistle."

Well, I was not sure how to handle the clippers but Grady showed me how and then had me clean the ground around a cross. It took me many Saturdays to get it done. All the while, I was on my quest for soda bottles to sell at the store. I began living on candy, cookies and chocolate milk. When they let me sleep indoors, it became a problem because I shared a room with my two sisters. I had to come up with a plan. In the bathroom was a closet for storing towels and such. Nancy had it packed with the good towels, towels no one ever used. I shoved my goodies underneath and to the back of the towels. Just before bed, I would go to the bathroom and woof them down.

Grady became my weekend treat. After a time I started visiting him three or four times a week. Nancy's newest boyfriend started taking her out often and for a few days at a time. Ellen had lost her job so she was home all the time and back in charge, giving me freedom to visit Grady as often as I wanted too.

Grady would tell me about his life and I slowly began telling him about my life but remembering to keep the secrets. We had such fun and began clearing the entire graveyard from the grass. I did not really pay attention at the time but Grady never did any real work and just talked to me and taught me how to survive. He always made me vow never, ever to tell anyone about him or the relationship we shared.

When the end of summer and talk of going back to school was everyone's topic the entire graveyard was cleaned. Every blade of grass cut back and the bushes trimmed. Grady showed me how to get sticks to support some of the collapsing crosses. I noticed that nearly every cross with the exception of few had no names or any writing on them.

I asked, "Shouldn't it say that somebody lies here?"

Grady replied, "These men threw their lives away and ruined the lives of their families all for the greed of gold. They are forgotten souls who had hard lessons to learn. At the end of their next life, their grave will have a name on it."

Well, I did not understand what he meant, so I said, "Monday is Labor day. I'll bring a picnic lunch of cookies and milk for us to share."
Grady smiled that wrinkled smile and embraced me as he said, "Remember never tell anyone about me."

I ran off for home feeling so happy with my friend and very proud of how we cleaned up that little cemetery.

That Sunday night, Nancy announced that she wanted to go to the beach for Labor day. I gasped in utter shock! I could not go, Grady would be waiting for me and I could not tell anyone.

The next morning I protested, saying I was ill and that I did not want to go but it seemed the more I protested something, the more it was enforced. So, away I went for a family outing. Finally, we had a family outing like normal people and I did not want to go. I was miserable all day, food was in abundance and I did not even have my purse with me to stock up.

That night when I went to bed, I prayed to Grady and apologized for not meeting him for our picnic lunch. The next day was school and that Saturday my father arrived and even though I was happy to see my father, he kept me away from Grady.

That Sunday I nearly ran the whole way to the cemetery but Grady was not there. I waited all day and he never showed up but there was three empty coke bottles on the bench.

I never saw Grady again but I kept taking care of the graveyard. I always hid the clippers under a bunch of leaves within the bushes. The nights became shorter and when it was cold and rainy I could not go to the graveyard at all.

A few years later, as I went to do my gardening at the cemetery, I stood devastated. There was a huge tractor parked, the ground turned over and not one single cross stood. The other section of the cemetery was in perfect condition but my cemetery was gone. There was no one for me to ask what happened. It was the weekend and there were no workers about. I sat there and cried my eyes out. I imagine that Grady had probably gotten sick and died. I had my broken cookies with me and I left them instead of flowers not knowing where they buried Grady or if he was even dead. My heart broke to lose him.

When I told my current husband about all about Grady, he did not believe me. I felt rather stunned that he did not believe me. Of course, my loving husband was kind and considerate in his tone as he expressed his opinion. I had shared Grady with no one and because I loved my husband so much I wanted him to know about Grady. Could it be that I imagined Grady, maybe he was a friend like Eddie-boy. Was I mad at the time? What was real and what was fantasy? No, Grady was real and my dear friend.

Chapter 9

I give up!

At nine years old lots of changes happened in my house. First, my mother's greatest fear happened. Sam received his draft notice. The fact was he was very happy about it but Nancy turned to prayer fearing the war. She was devastated thinking of what might happen to her precious boy.

Sam left early one morning leaving Nancy in tears. She immediately set up a shrine to Sam of which, candles were always lit and her ritual prayers done faithfully every night and every evening to be sure God watched over him. I suppose it was rather foolish because he was still in California doing Basic Training.

To add to Nancy's worries Hester started ditching school and going to "Boy Parties" until Hester got caught and arrested. She was caught by the police in a hotel room, naked. Apparently, she was the only girl in the hotel room with six boys, each taking their turn, if you know what I mean. I believe Hester simply felt starved for love and attention. I remember Hester asking Nancy once, "Why don't you ever hug us or kiss us and tell us you love us?"

Nancy's cold reply, "You can't ever miss

what you never had. I'm doing you a favor."

Hester was desperate to feel loved and found it the only why she knew how. By the time Hester was fifteen years old she ran away from home. Nancy felt devastated when she heard some months later that Hester was pregnant. A young man named Richard came to the house and addressed Nancy with his head held proud.

"I am Richard and I am here to ask permission to marry Hester. She is going to have my baby and I want to do the right thing by her."

Nancy looked at him with that hateful glare. She ranted and raved spewing out quotes from the bible. In the end, she gave her permission and signed a document giving Hester who was a minor, permission to marry. Richard left and months passed but Hester never returned.

Well, I was astounded because it was as simple as just leaving. Walking out the door never to return and that would be the end of all my suffering. If Hester could just leave then so could I, it really was as simple as that or so I thought. With me, nothing is ever simple. Nevertheless, I began my quest for freedom as I plotted and planned my escape. I put much thought in where I would go. I did realize I needed a way to make money to survive. What work could I get at my age?

At the time, I did not know that Ellen too was plotting and planning for an escape. Never having really put thought into it, I realize now that to a degree Hester and Ellen was also abused. I never really saw them get beat but Ellen was literary the housekeeper and when she was in school she often had to miss class to tend to the household chores. Hester, grew up frighten of Nancy and it was obvious that Hester was starved for a feeling of security and a desperate need to be loved. Years later, the consequences would surface as Hester became an alcoholic and Ellen became mean and bitter unable to find a relationship that would last.

Anyway, back to my escape, bright one morning while Nancy was still in bed I packed a change of clothes, my journal, my MoMo and put on a sweater. I tipped-toed out the door and was on my way to freedom. I decided the best thing for me to do was to find my Aunt Louisa, I always remembered her telling my father that I belonged with their family. Of course, I had no idea what direction to go or how far my destination would take me.

I walked and walked, stopping for short rests and regretting that I did not bring any food or a drink with me. I was such a fool, a naive fool that was bringing more misery than I had ever experienced to myself.

When it began to grow dark, I was cold and hungry. My surroundings did not look familiar. The truth was, I was lost and was not even sure how to return home. I saw a church and entered to get some warmth. It was so beautiful inside with lots of statues but for some reason it was rather scary to me. I sat on the last bench and just stared at the statue of Jesus Christ on the cross. A realization came to me a profound thought or an awakening of sorts. I buried my face into my MoMo and cried my eyes out.

A nun came up and sat next to me. “What’s happened, child? Where are your parents?”

I looked up and wiped my tears not having an answer to reply. She took my MoMo and asked, “How did his face get burned?”

I snatched my MoMo back from her and replied, “Nancy burned him...” I could not continue for tears now possessed me.

The nun held me in her arms and said almost in a whisper, “I am Sister Margaret. You did well by coming here to God’s house. You are safe.”

I pulled back as anger surged through me. I shouted causing echoes throughout the church, “Safe... like him... bleeding on the cross! God didn’t help his son, why would he help me!”

I ran out of the church as fast as I could. I kept running and running even though I could hardly catch my breath. Now, I understood why my prayers went unanswered; God was just like Nancy. He held all the power and yet he allowed his only son to be tortured and hung on a cross. Even now, there hangs his son’s body, bleeding and dying in his house for all to see. *God hates me as much as Nancy does... who do I go to for help? Why is this happening?* These were the thoughts that raced through my brain when suddenly, red lights flashed as a siren went on and off. I came to a stop panting from exhaustion. There behind me, and along side of me was the POLICE! I had done it now, jail is what awaited me and now I had my own cross to bear.

A police officer came up to me and squatted down, "Where you off to missy? What's your name... is it Rebecca Marie Mendez?"

Sister Margaret came up to me and took my hand. "Don't worry child. Let the policeman help you."

She spoke like an angel but angels and such had a different meaning for me now. My whole outlook on life took on a different meaning. The fact was I was alone in my struggle to survive and along the way I had demons to battle.

The policeman repeated the questions and I nodded identifying myself. He escorted me to the back seat of his car. Sister Margaret made the sign of the cross and held her rosary beads, it disgusted me to see her pretending to care. They took me to the police department. I sat in a little office until a social worker came in and questioned me as to why I was running away and what was happening in my home.

For the most part, I did not give any answers, just shrugged and nodded as I hung my head waiting to go to prison. Then, they left me to sit alone in the office where I eventually fell asleep. I woke when Nancy nudged me. There in front of everyone she put on her show. "Oh my goodness Rebecca Marie I was so worried about you. Why did you run away? What would I do without you?"

After her performance was over, they released me to Nancy and off we went for home. Emotionally, I was numb and felt empty inside. I did not even have God to pray to anymore. In addition, Eddie-boy was not even present as I was ushered into the garage.

Nancy ranted and raved for what seemed like hours on end. Exhaustion was overwhelming to the point I was not even paying attention to what she was saying. As usual, I sat on the stool, on my hands with my bare feet on the cold concrete floor. My head hung down to my chest as her screaming continued. I did not realize when Nancy picked up the mallet or took notice when she lifted it up but I did see when it came down on my feet. Before I could react, it came down again. For a second or two I was shocked then the pain...the horrible pain. I fell off the stool on my right side and the mallet came down again hitting the side of my left foot. I think I screamed. Ellen ran into the garage and saw Nancy with the mallet over my head ready to let it drop on me again but she shouted, "Mama NO!"

Nancy looked at Ellen then at me. She set down the mallet and simply walked out of the garage. Ellen went up to me and looked at my feet.

"You stupid fool, why the hell did you try to run away? Just do what you're told and keep your mouth shut. When you are eighteen you can leave."

Ellen left the garage and left me shaking and crying on the floor feeling such pain that I cannot even describe. I tried to get up but any movement shot hot sharp pain through my throbbing feet. Eddie-boy finally appeared and handed me my MoMo. He held me and cried with me.

Despite how tried I felt, I did not sleep a wink that night from the pain. At first light, I heard Nancy's slippers shuffle to her Sam Shrine, where I knew she was praying. Then, I heard her turn on the peculator for morning coffee. I looked at my black swollen feet and ankles knowing they had to be broken. I heard the click of the door handle and there she stood. She walked over to me and said, "Try and run away again and see what you get."

She squatted down and examined my feet. "You are not going to be running anywhere for a long time." She said that with almost a chuckle to her tone.

That day forever burned in my memory as Nancy took it upon herself to be doctor and nurse. She made splints and set my feet and ankles using lots of ace bandages. She got out Hester's old crutches and told me, "Use the crutches if you need to go to the bathroom. Otherwise, just stay on your sleeping bag. Here... swallow this."

She handed me a pill, I didn't know or care what it was, I just didn't care about anything anymore. I swallowed the pill and drank down the glass of water she gave me. Shortly after, I was in a deep sleep. I did not wake until nearly dawn the next day. I was hungry and in terrible pain. I cried because that is all I could do. I do not know how long it took my feet to heal; I never saw a doctor or had an X-Ray. Months passed and I missed a good deal of school and was grossly behind in my studies. But what was worst during my healing time I only got to eat a few times a week so I was skin and bones and extremely weak.

The return to school was hard for me, even though it appeared that my feet were healed they still ached terribly. I had no clue what the teacher was taking about in regards to my lessons. The kids tormented me with their mean insults and my present teacher had no interest in my problems. I do not even think she knew if I was in her class until the day I fainted.

I was sitting in class, feeling hungry and tired when everything went quiet then black. I fainted dead away. I woke in the nurse's office. This nurse was older and seemed a little cranky, not like the way I remembered Miss Green.

She took my temperature then placed her hands on her hips. "Well what is wrong with you? Are you sick?"

I looked at her thinking, *You are the nurse...*

Surely, you can tell that I am not feeling well. But if you really want to know, I am sick and tired of my home, school and my life. Of course, I just shook my head in reply and had no words to offer.

When, I felt a little better, she told me to go back to class. At this point in my life, I had no outward emotions. I nearly never spoke, mostly due to my stuttering. I was taking speech classes but they did not seem to work and after missing so much school, I felt like a lost cause. My journals were more elaborate now that I could read and write to a certain degree. Everything was probably misspelled and I am sure there was no grammar to speak of but I wrote in my journal diligently. I was upset that I had forgotten my journal in Sister Margaret's church the day I ran away. I assumed she looked at all the evil writing in it and threw it in the trash. What I did not know was that after she read it she turned it over to the social worker who placed it in my file.

Starving was all I seemed to be about that year. I began fainting a lot and the worst was when I tried to eat it made me sick and quite often I would vomit or just have dry-heaves. Food and the lack of it became a nightmare. I had no freedom to go out and collect Pop bottles to buy broken cookies. I was at the mercy of Nancy and she had none.

Then, the day came when Ellen said good-bye. She had been corresponding with companies for work and got a job in Reno, Nevada as a casino cashier. She and her friend were going to share an apartment. Nancy was angry going on and on about the sinful life she was going to fall too. Nevertheless, Ellen was now over twenty-one years old and Nancy could not stop her.

Ellen waved to me "Good luck kid." I waved back envying her, her freedom. I watched Ellen and her friend walk off for the bus stop carrying their suitcases as happy as they could be. Now, it was just Nancy and me.

That evening Nancy got good and drunk, she called me names, "You filthy little nigger. All I did for my kids and I end up stuck with you. If it weren't for the child support check, I would have killed you long ago. Look at you with that frizzy hair and those black devil eyes."

I sat without saying a word listening to her go on about Sam, Hester and Ellen having all abandoned her. She finally fell to a drunken stupor and passed out on the couch. I went to bed assuming it was Okay to sleep in the house. I did not care if she kicked me out later. Maybe if she killed me, she and I would be better off. Eddie-boy, MoMo and I slept in the warm bed on clean sheets. When I woke, Nancy was at her Sam Shrine doing her morning prayers. I quietly went to the bathroom to wash then I got dressed. Nancy called me into the living room.

"Damn ungrateful kids! I have to get a job. The money your father sends will not be enough.

He was sending me enough but now that my kids are gone, he is only going to send me enough money for your worthless ass. I'll be out all day. It's now your job to clean the house and do the ironing."

With that, she got all dressed up and left. Well, this wasn't so bad I was home alone. I turned the TV on and began sweeping, dusting and doing the dishes. I liked to listen to the TV while I did house work. This was fun. This I could deal with. I really did not know how to do anything but I gave it my best try. I made myself a baloney sandwich, big mistake. I puked it all up. It's strange to explain but I was so hungry that I could not eat. I could not tolerate the smell of food or the taste of it. I was so weak and tired all the time and began to notice a fine downy hair on my arms and legs.

Nancy came home late that night with a hamburger and fries for herself. She walked around the house to see if I did my chores then she told me to go to the garage. Darn, I had hoped I could sleep in the warm house. After about an hour or so, she walked into the garage with a stick in her hand.

"I have to clean disgusting old people, to pay the mortgage payment and the bills. I have to work at the most nasty place you can imagine to put a roof over your head. You are a costly burden to me!"

I shrank in the corner understanding her tone of voice and waited for the stick to come down on me. She beat me mercilessly that night. I think she only stopped because she got tired. The garage was dark so I could not tell how bad my beating was but pain once again found a home in my body. I felt my swollen eyes stinging from the tears. As always, Eddie-boy was there to comfort me.

The next morning, I heard Nancy slam the front door; start up her car and leave. I assumed she was going to her new job. I went to the kitchen door and opened it. I got a drink of water then went to the bathroom where I looked into the mirror in horror. She did it again, my face was bruised and swollen, I had a fat-lip and a black eye. I looked at my arms and legs taking notice of all the bruising. It angered me, so much, so that I thought about trying to run away again. But where could I go? I had to think this through. I thought about my Aunt Louisa again, that was the only place I could think of but I now understood that I could not just walk there. I remembered that Ellen went to the bus stop.

I dug through the house for loose change and came up with sixteen cents. I collected empty coke bottles, put them in a big bag and then dressed warmly. This was it; just like Hester and Ellen, I was getting the hell out of here.

I went to the market to sell the bottles and received seventy-five cents. I asked the box-boy how I could get to Oakland. He told me what corner to go to, to catch the bus.

Deeply concerned, the grocer asked, "What

happened to you Rebecca Marie? Do you need a doctor? Did your mother do this to you?"

I simply replied, "I fell down the stairs." With that, I ran off to catch the bus.

I stood at the Bus stop waiting and watching for it to come when Nancy drove up and said through clenched teeth, "Get into this car at once!" It was obvious that I was running away again, I had a bag with a change of clothes and my MoMo with me.

Now she would surely kill me. I got into the car and we drove home in silence. Once home, I ran into the garage and waited for what would happen next.

After a long while passed, Nancy entered the garage and told me to sit on my stool, barefooted. I sat there as she ordered me to close my eyes. When I did not close my eyes, she smacked me so hard I flew off the stool. She repeated her order and I of course did as ordered. Once again, Nancy took the mallet to my feet until I passed out.

The next day she tended to my broken feet, I can only assume they were broken I never went to the doctor. After a few days, some of my toenails fell off. Forced to stay home from school to heal I did not expect to live through this new ordeal. I did my household chores during the day as I hobbled through the house. Hunger and illness plagued me, I often got cold sweats and eating simply became impossible. Sometimes I would faint and just lay on the floor until I regained consciousness. No one was there to help me.

All I thought about was, "Where in the hell is my father?"

Nancy started drinking heavily on a daily bases and beating me became a way for her to vent her frustrations. She hated her job. However, she had to work to survive.

As for me, I gave up. There was no escape for me and I had to simply endure or die.

My immediate salvation was school. I had not been to school in a very long time and so a truant officer came to the door early one day when I was home alone. I opened the door and needless to say, he looked at me shocked by my appearance. "What happened to you? Are you Rebecca Mendez?"

I was so ill that day. I felt so frail and sick to my stomach. I think I identified myself to him. I do not really remember what happened. All that comes to mind was opening the door to the truant officer.

The next thing I knew I was in an ambulance. The sirens going wild, a man telling me to stay awake and to talk to him, it was madness. I was in a daze and sleep now forced my eyes shut. I woke next in a hospital bed hooked up to tubes and upside down bottles. I was in and out of a daze not understanding if hours or days were passing. When I was fully awake, I wore bandages on my legs and feet. They gave me Jell-O but I just could not eat it.

Later, I nurse handed me a cup of broth which I was able to hold down. Then, the questioning began by a man and woman. I do not remember their names. Suddenly, she appeared... it was Mrs. Castora.

Mrs. Castora held my journal that I had left at Sister Margaret's church. "Rebecca, I have read your diary. I know what you have been going through. Let me help you get away from your mother before she kills you. I could not help you the last time because you would not tell the truth. If you tell the truth now you can go and live with the Crugers and stay there until you are grown up. Help me to help you."

Well, she read my journal and I thought at this stage what did I have to lose. I truthfully answered all the questions to the best of my ability. I spent a couple of weeks in the hospital and ate soup, crackers and jell-O. Mrs. Castora was there to pick me up when upon my discharged. Away I went to the Cruger family. They were so happy to have me back. The little girls they had before had been replaced with new little girls. I felt at home, at long last at home. I could stay here safe and in comfort.

Sometime later, I am not sure how much time but I had to go to court. I found out that Nancy was arrested and was now struggling with the law to get herself out of trouble. I did not care, I was going to live with the Crugers now and be happy. I do not even know why they made me go to court. Mrs. Castora took the stand and argued in my defense telling the court that it was in my best interest to remain in the care of the Crugers who could give me stability and love. The Crugers were there with me and it made me feel safe from Nancy's evil stares. She did as usual putting on her performance but I knew that Mrs. Castora would not believe her. I was free and going home with the Crugers.

Suddenly, Mrs. Castora shouted, "You can't... if she goes back Miss VanBuren is sure to kill her. Please, your honor, don't do this to that poor little girl!"

I was rather startled at the outburst and not really understanding until the Judge ordered, "Release Rebecca Marie Mendez to her mother. Miss VanBuren is taking all the proper steps to correct her situation. It's in the child's best interest to stay with her biological mother."

Mrs. Castora continued to protest but to no avail. The Crugers hugged me and told me they were sorry I had to go. I began crying and yelling in protest to stay with the Crugers. Nevertheless, my fate was sealed and I went home with Nancy.

Chapter 10

I'm Needed

My life changed once I was home. Nancy had to stop hurting me if she wanted to avoid jail and now a social worker would come randomly once a week to check on me. I also had many doctors' appointments to attend, weekly iron shots and B vitamin shots. The nurse always weighed me and questioned me as to how I was doing. Nancy had to be sure I ate three times a day and menu diaries had to be kept. Although, they sent me back to my hell, they did not leave me alone with Nancy, so to spcak.

The verbal abused continued more severely because it was the only thing she could do to me without anyone knowing about it. Looking back, I can see that she destroyed every bit of my self-esteem and made me feel ashamed of my body.

Things were somewhat better in school too, since I was so far behind in my studies I was allowed to use the library as much as I wanted to, to try and catch up. This meant I by-passed all recess for study taking myself away from the bullies.

That fall, my father came to visit me and buy me school clothes. Then, to my delight, the long awaited trip finally happened. He took me to visit my Aunt Louisa. She was so happy to see me and made such a big fuss as to how beautiful I looked. She scolded my father for keeping me away from my family. It felt so good to be thought of as part of her family. The visit was short but very enjoyable.

I do not know if my father knew about all that had happened to me. He never said a word and neither did I, there just seemed no point in telling him. I guess if he knew he did not really care. He arrived on Sunday afternoon. He pulled a brand new bike from the trunk of his car and told me it was an early Christmas present.

Well, I was overjoyed to say the least. The bike had a basket on the handlebars and my first thought was I could run errands to the store for Nancy. It was a very happy day. As usual, my father visited me for a few Sundays and then he was off to sea again. This time I did not cry and beg for him to take me with him. I had given up the fight and accepted my situation.

Part of the new routine the doctors set for me was exercise so Nancy had to allow me to ride my bike as much as I wanted too. She really did not seem to mind and I often went to the store for her to fetch, soda pop, candy and items needed for meals and such. I remember running those errands with joy liking that I could place the items in my basket and ride home feeling the wind on my face. However, like everything in my life, that gave me joy, it was short lived.

Nancy had her friends over to play a game of cards and she sent me to the market to buy a six-pack of coke. I jumped on my bike, rolled down the slope of the driveway and through two parked cars... then directly into a passing car. I remember the event in a blur as the passing car's door handle and my handle bar seemed to be stuck, me and my bike were dragged a few feet before I fell to the ground banging my head on the bumper then on the ground.

My bike was destroyed and my head split open. Once again, I was in the emergency room whereupon they drilled Nancy as to what happened. I do not know the details but I got many stitches in my head and suffered a concussion. The driver of the car explained what happened and Nancy was free of any wrongdoing. It was an accident pure and simple.

Over the next few days, I suffered vertigo and severe headaches along with a stiff neck. I believe I had a neck injury too but in that day and age, they overlooked it. I suffered severe neck pain for many years but as always, I recovered and moved on with my life, minus a bicycle.

For my twelfth birthday, Mrs. Castora brought me a cake on her regular visit. She sang happy birthday to me and gave me a package of lacy handkerchiefs. She was such an angel to me and I grew to love her very much. My thirteenth year I went off to Junior High where my self-esteem issue worsened. I had the body of a small boy and the girls in gym class wore sexy panties and bras. They laughed at me because I had no need for a bra. I hated gym class where I had to remove my clothes and wear shorts in front of everyone. Nancy always forbid me to remove my clothes in front of other people or wear shorts.

At home, I became an asset to Nancy. It was my job to keep the house clean and in proper order. I ran her errands without hesitation or protest. I learned quickly that every task had to be done immediately without hesitation. Nancy hated it when she had to repeat herself. I became her emotionalist, empty-hearted drone. Nevertheless, it was Okay with me. I ate regularly now and was not beat anymore. The insults and bad words hurt but I dealt with it. Eddie-boy was only an occasionally visitor now but I still slept with my MoMo.

One bright day, Hester entered the house with a cute little girl and a precious little baby in her arms. She placed the baby in my arms, "Rebecca Marie you are so grown up. These are my children Tina and Josh."

I looked at the baby that I held in my arms and smiled from ear to ear. This was the first baby I had ever held. Richard told me, "Josh is your nephew and Tina is your Niece. Tina this is your Aunt Rebecca."

I looked at Richard stunned that he said I

was his children's Aunt. I felt tears flood my eyes with such joy but as always my joy was short lived. Nancy hated Richard as much as she hated me. "Rebecca Marie is not my grandchildren's Aunt! They can just call her Rebecca Marie."

Richard looked at me and glared at Nancy with obvious hate. He seemed like such a nice man but later I would find out different. Anyway, I left the room and went to my bedroom. I sat on my bed and held my MoMo. I could hear them talking in the next room. Nancy continuously insulted Richard. It sounded like she truly loved her grandchildren, especially Tina. I began writing in my journal when Tina walked into my room. She walked up to me, so cute in her smart little dress. "Hi Tina," I said with a bright smile.

Tina was very little and did not speak much yet. She smiled at me then ran out of the room. She probably got scared when she looked at my black devil eyes. I felt bad for scaring her. I went back to writing in my journal. It was easier for me to hide my journals now since I did all the housework. The couple of times Nancy found my journals in the past was not an experience I wanted to repeat. Yet, I felt drawn to writing in my journals even if it meant I had to burn them to be sure they were not read by anyone.

That Christmas, I sat alone watching "A Christmas Carol" on the television. Nancy had to work the swing shift now, which was nice because I could watch all the TV I wanted.

At midnight, I looked out the window and whispered, "Merry Christmas Daddy, merry Christmas Tina. Merry Christmas, Mrs. Castora."

I had two presents under the tree, one from my Daddy and one from Mrs. Castora. Because Mrs. Castora was keeping a close eye on me, my presents were mine to open and keep.

Mrs. Castora package had gloves, handkerchiefs and the prettiest little purse I had ever seen. My father sent me a charm bracelet and a twenty-dollar bill. I put the bracelet on thinking it was the prettiest thing I ever owned. After I went to bed, I thought it was strange that Nancy had not come home yet. Morning came and not a word. The phone rang and Mr. Garduno, Nancy's boss said, "Rebecca, are you all right? Your mother had an accident. She'll be home soon."

I told him I was fine and thanked him for calling. I wondered what kind of accident she could have been in. A couple of hour's later two cars drove up. One car was Nancy's driven by Mr. Garduno and the other car was a big shiny black car driven by a lady. The couple helped Nancy out of the car, up to the porch where I stood with the door open. Nancy looked dazed and wore a cast on her arm.

The lady gave me a bag with a burger, fries and a milkshake then explained, "Your mother fell at work and broke her arm. She needs to sleep right now. If you need anything give us a call."

I thanked her for the food and watched her put Nancy to bed. After they left, I checked on Nancy who was out cold. I shut her bedroom door and went to the living room to watch TV; another version of the Christmas Carol was going to be on. I enjoyed the movie as I gobbled up my burger and fries. From years of being condition to eat fast before they took my plate away from me, I now ate my food without thought, gobbling it down quickly. To this day, I have trouble controlling that habit.

When the sun went down Nancy called out to me. I ran to her bedroom where she was in tears telling me she had to go to the bathroom but could hardly move. Her cast covered her hand, arm and up passed the elbow, a bar of shorts held her arm up at shoulder level. It looked uncomfortable. As I helped her up, she let out a stream of obscenities. I felt so sorry that she was in so much pain.

Once in the bathroom she ordered me out. I could hear her cursing terribly as I imagined how she could tend to her toilet needs in such a position. After a while, she came out and demanded her pills, which I gave her. Then I ran to the kitchen and heated up some chicken noodle soup. When I got back with the tray, she was in a dead sleep again.

I became Nancy's caretaker but you know what, I loved every moment of it. She still spoke to me in a belittling manner but now she needed me and I saw to her every need. I combed her hair, brought her food and helped her dress. I brought her wash water because she simply could not take a bath. I ran her errands and felt filled with joy.

Christmas Vacation ended and I had to go back to School. Children's social services forbid me by state law to miss school without a doctor's note. Nancy had to be on her own during the day. Eventual they removed the bar she wore and now she hung her arm in a sling. The cast was still awkward. I wished she would wear it for the rest of her life so I could go on taking care of her.

Sam came home for a visit, he was out of the army now and married but he was a self-centered bastard and as mean as he could be. He offered no help to Nancy when she needed it most, not even offering a ride to the doctor. For a while, Mr. Garduno saw to Nancy getting to the doctor but one day, he and Nancy argued terribly.

I found out Nancy was suing Mr. Garduno and wanting many thousands of dollars for her injury. Her worker's compensation paid her $105 per month and the mortgage was $98 leaving her nearly nothing for utilities bills and food. To make matters worse my Daddy seemed to have fallen off the grid so to speak; no money came and no word.

Hiding and lying from bill collectors was all Nancy and I did. She asked Ellen, Sam and Hester for money but they all refused. She could not get a job with a cast on her arm and she could not drive the car either. I ran all her errands for her using

Ellen's old bike or if it was raining, I took the bus. That summer, I walked into the house and found Nancy crying her heart out. There was no food, no money and it looked like she had no more hope.

I got an idea and left her knowing just how to make her smile. I took out Sam's old red wagon and went through the neighbor's trash looking for Soda pop bottles. I filled the wagon and took off to the market to sell the bottles. Then, I went out, refilled the wagon with more pop bottles and sold those bottles too. I ran home, put the wagon away and ran into the house panting for air.

Nancy spat, "What the hell is wrong with you? You are no good..."

I simply held out my hand, showing her ten one dollar bills. Shocked she gasped, "Where did you get that money?"

I happily told her just how I earned the money. She took the money with a great smile. Then she walked with me to the store where we bought some groceries. I pointed out her favorite candy." Don't you think you should get a couple of Baby Ruth bars?"

Nancy happily nodded. I felt like life could not get better. I made Nancy happy! That night we had dinner together on TV trays in front of the TV. She told me about when she was a little girl and performed at talent shows. It was the best day of my life. After that day, I would go neighbor to neighbor offering to clean house, do ironing, babysit or run errands to earn money. As always, I would take a wagonload of bottles to the store. One day after everyone paid me, I handed Nancy twenty-five dollars, whereupon she paid the power bill and was able to turn the phone service back on.

The lawyer came over to talk to Nancy and explained to her that Mr. Garduno had an investigator watching her. "Our claim is that you are so handicapped that you can't work, drive or even take care of yourself. We can win if you play the game right. Do not doubt for a minute that they will be watching you. You might get a fake salesman come to your door in hopes of catching you doing a function that you should not be able to do, like lifting something. In addition don't think someone won't take a picture of your activities. You must prove that you are helpless. Stay on your guard and we'll both make a lot of money."

The summer of my fourteenth was by far the most exciting in my childhood. I learned to drive. Nobody, my age could drive. Nancy grew restless being home all the time. Therefore, I became her chauffeur. She did not have a cast on her arm any more but she always acted like her arm was dead weight. She instructed me on the fundamentals of driving. It was so much fun. I had some trouble with the breaks forcing us to jerk forward then back. Within a short period, I was DRIVING! It was summertime, I got a job at Arla's Burgers and Malts, and every evening I would bring Nancy home goodies to eat from work.

I would drive Nancy around in the evenings wherever she wanted to go. Weekends, we went to the new Southland Mall, and did window-shopping before stopping at the Doggy Dinner for hot dogs and Grape soda. We actually talked. Nancy loved to watch people and tell me how ugly or fat or strange they looked.

One day when we were in Woolworth's Department store a girl I knew from school joined us for a milkshake. We talked and laughed about fashion, shoes and gossip. Nancy was like a friend and it made me feel so good when my friend said, "Rebecca, your mom is so cool. I wish my mom was like yours." I could tell that statement also made Nancy happy.

That fall, my father still did not return and there were no new school clothes. Most of the clothes I had from the year before were too small. Therefore, together Nancy and I made me a few dresses and skirts. Nancy was an excellent seamstress and she insisted that I learn to sew. "You have to be able to do something in your life. You can't always depend on me, you know," she said.

Once I was back in school, I had little time to take care of Nancy. After school, I went straight to work and did not get home until ten o'clock. I always worked on Saturdays and took overtime if I could get it. Nancy's lawsuit was taking forever and so it was necessary for me to work.

Mrs. Castora only came for visits once every two months now, as ordered by the court. That November, Nancy had fulfilled her probation. Nancy firmly told Mrs. Castora that she was not welcome in her house anymore. Nevertheless, for years, Mrs. Castora visited me at school, or the library just to check on me. I loved her so much. She was truly an angel.

That Christmas, money only covered the bills. We had no Christmas tree and very little food. On December 22, the phone rang and I answered it. "TeeTee, it's Daddy."

I nearly gasped as I said "Daddy, is it really you!"

Nancy heard me, grabbed the phone out of my hand and started an argument with my father. That night in the rain he came to the house whereupon, Nancy told him we were starving to death and did not even have a Christmas tree.

My father took both of us to dinner where Nancy ordered the most expensive plate. Then, at the grocery store, we filled a cart with food and at the exit; my father bought us a Christmas tree. He did not have presents for me that year but gave me a one-hundred dollar bill. He apologized a million times for being away for so long. I think he gave Nancy all the back child support he owed because when he handed her a check her eyes lit up. I knew all too well that look on her face when she was happy with the amount of money.

February was the big court case to Nancy and her lawyer's dismay. Pictures of Nancy hanging the laundry on the backyard clothesline and, pictures of her lifting the basket with wet clothes and even raking leaves were on display.

The apricot orchard behind us was leveled and apartments built. From the top floor of the apartments was a clear view of our backyard. Mr. Garduno's investigator took pictures of Nancy tending to many chores while I was away at school or work.

Nancy lost her court case and only her medical bills were paid. When we were back home, the devil returned. Nancy was mean and cruel. She did not have to fake limits anymore and Mrs. Castora was no longer in the picture.

Nancy was no fool, she only returned to smacking me upside the head or hitting me on my body so no one could see marks. She needed me to continue working because she needed the money. Cruel verbal abuse and whipping me with a stick on my back-end returned. I was a young lady now and she was sure to remind me how ugly and disgusting my body was, a sinful thing to hide and keep covered. I believed her and always wore long sleeves and high collars. My skirts were never above my knee. I was quiet, distant and withdrew often to my little fantasy world and my journals that I now filled with fictional events that I could only dream about.

Chapter 11

Grown up

When I reached my sixteenth year, Hester returned home, having left Richard. She claimed he was always drunk and often beat her. I was surprised to hear that Richard could behave in such a manner; he always seemed so nice.

Once Hester was in the house, I became her housekeeper and babysitter whenever I was home. Her time in Nancy's house was short, having found a new husband within a period of six months or so. No sooner did Hester leave when Ellen returned home with her baby boy.

Ellen was bitter, and mean. Her husband had her committed for a time after she had a nervous breakdown. When they released from the hospital, she left him and returned to Nancy. Ellen did not allow me to babysit her son or even hold him. She always looked at me as if I were a freak. I now slept on the couch because Ellen wanted a room to herself and the other room was for her baby boy.

Nancy made me get up real early and clean up the living room saying, "I don't like it to look like a bedroom. This is the living room after all."

School was a nightmare of torment from the girls. They laughed at me and called me names and then there was Gym class where the arguing would start because nobody wanted me on their team for fear that would lose whatever sport we were playing. Where boys were concerned, I was painfully shy, misunderstanding, the boys called me a snob or stuck-up, saying, "Oh you think you are too good for me."

My studies were poor, like my grades but writing was my passion. However, my grammar skills were terrible. Years of malnutrition and most likely all the injuries to my head caused me to have a poor memory which brought about learning disabilities like not being able to remember rules of grammar, spelling and how to process math problems.

Nevertheless, my goal was to be a famous writer one day. I wrote a story for a class assignment feeling proud of it as I read it over and over again. After I turned it in, I waited for days on pins and needles wanting to see what my grade would be. When my English teacher returned my paper to me, it had a big RED "F" on it. She made so many corrections the paper looked like it bled.

After class, I walked up to her and asked, "I know my grammar and spelling are bad but what did you think about my story?"

The English teacher returned, "Rebecca, you wrote a science fiction story… girls don't write such dribble. Your characters are uninteresting and downright evil. The violence is offensive! You write empty words. Read books for entertainment but for your future find yourself a good husband or maybe you can work at the cannery."

Her words tore into me like a jagged blade. My heart broke from the disappointment as I fought back tears. Again, I failed. I was useless. I did not write a fictional story again until I was thirty-eight years old.

I did not realize it then but by my seventeenth year, I was an attractive young lady. A late bloomer, true, but now as I looked back at pictures, I was in fact pretty. An art teacher in my school approached me, asking if I would pose for his photography class. I just shook my head in embarrassment but he was persistent and told me he would give me copies of the pictures. I could not understand why he wanted pictures of me. He convinced me and there I stood awkward as he and his students took the pictures.

A week later, he showed me the proofs and said, "You'd make a great model. You are a little short and your facial features are not balanced but you are very beautiful Rebecca with those bewitching black eyes." I blushed, feeling as if he might be laughing at me.

I told Nancy about it and of course, she thought he was some pervert attracted to me because I was acting like a slut. Once I got my period, "Slut" became her favorite word to call me. I was far from being a slut but knew better than to protest or talk back.

Nancy got a job as a seamstress for a short while, but hating work she quit. I do not know how she got money to pay the bills but with my check and what she collected, the bills were paid. This was a time that Nancy had many boyfriends and they would often stay nights at the house. On those occasions, she locked me in the garage. I was five foot seven inches tall now and that dirty old sleeping bag that had nearly come apart when I tried to wash it, was awkward to sleep on. What choice did I have, I dealt with it.

On workdays, Nancy was sure to let me out of the garage in time for work. I have to say it was ridiculous that she locked me in the garage. I often wondered if Nancy was jealous of me, possibly she thought the men she brought home would be attracted to me. Or, maybe in her own crazy way she just wanted to protect me. One boyfriend came and never left, he was nice and respectful to me and I could tell this man was here to stay. He had many friends one of which was going to drastically change my life but I'll get to that later.

Nancy's family seemed to warm up to me somewhat as I became a young woman. Many of my cousins were getting married. Since we were a Catholic family these weddings were big. I loved it when a cousin asked me to be her bridesmaid. It was my chance to wear beautiful gowns, with matching shoes and sometimes a large brimmed hat. It was all so exciting. True I had to work extra hours to pay for the gowns but that was all right with me. On occasions, my Daddy helped me out and made the purchase for me.

At the wedding receptions, Nancy gave me permission to only socialize and dance with family. Nancy was like a hawk keeping an eye that I not speak or dance with someone she did not know. Each wedding reception was the same. I really did not care, I still had fun but it bothered me that she did not trust me. Never had I disobeyed any of her orders and I always went out of my way for her, yet she had this idea that the moment she turned her back I would run off like Hester did.

My teenage years were busy, filled with taking care of Nancy's home, work and school. There were times during the summers when I had two jobs. I was always tired but felt like at least I was pulling my weight. I did not want to be a burden to Nancy who always complained about how expensive it was to feed me and see to my medical needs.

This was a time when I took to sneaking shots of Tequila. It was wrong, but sometimes I felt so tired that I could not sleep and I found that a shot or two helped me relax. I was clever about it and never got caught. I do not believe I was an alcoholic but I did have a drink or two nearly every day.

Christmas my father bought me a brand new three-speed bike. This was great! I could use my bike to go to work and save money. With no bus fair to pay, I could buy lipstick and mascara. Nancy did not care if I used makeup so long as it was respectable and I bought it myself. Working at Martin's Variety store (a five and dime) I now could make purchases at an employee's discount. I excitedly bought stockings, makeup and even perfume. In addition, just to smooth the way, I always bought Nancy a pair of stockings too. She loved getting gifts and I really enjoyed it when she looked happy.

Nevertheless, there were days when Nancy was in one of her moods. Since her boyfriend Louie lived in the house with us, my beatings were in secret. She did not want him to know or give him a chance to interfere. She would wait until he was at work, just out, or when he was asleep. I would go out to the garage and wait to see what the instrument of punishment would be.

I hated the switch/cane the most because not only did it sting terribly but the sound it made as it whoosh through the air and whack against my flesh terrified me. To make matters worse being a young woman, the humiliation went deeper. Now, I had breasts and when Nancy made me bare them was even worse than when she forced me to bare my buttocks. We were alone thereby no witnesses but it was still degrading for me.

Once she swung the belt and struck me across my breasts with a mighty wallop! The pain was so intense I froze for a moment unable to breath. When tears came to my eyes, Nancy laughed and smacked me upside the head. I swear she took a great deal of pleasure in punishing me.

Nancy took care not to mark my legs or arms and most especially my face. However, there were those times when I guarded my face or tried to cover the place I thought she might strike me and sure enough, I got a welt and/or bruise where it would show. This made her angrier worsening my situation. When people asked, I simply responded with, "I fell" everyone was aware of how clumsy and nervous I was so no one thought anything unusual of my appearance.

What really upset me was my uncontrollable reaction to protect myself from the strikes, a reaction that got me into more trouble. To this day, it is always my reaction to put my hand up to guard myself even-though I know there is no threat of me being hurt.

The art teacher at school always asked me to pose for his photography class, they were respectable photos in a high school atmosphere but I refused telling him the truth, "My mother doesn't approve. I can't do it."

Mr. Hill, continued to be persistent and I have to admit I liked how he would come up to me and compliment me on my appearance. I did not understand at the time but now as I think back he might have been flirting with me. I was naive and disregarded his advances. Mr. Hill took steps into his own hands and contacted Mrs. Warren from a Modeling agency. Apparently, he showed her some of the pictures he took of me. Mrs. Warren approached me after school one day and identified herself. She gave me her business card and told me she would like to be my agent. She went on and on as I stood stunned thinking this was nuts... *me a model?*

I went home, told Nancy all about it and

gave her Mrs. Warren's card. Nancy looked at me, letting her eyes go up and down visually examining me from head to toe. She told Louie about Mrs. Warren and he enthusiastically said, "I told you she was a beauty. Let her model she'll make a ton of money."

It was rather overwhelming for me when I received compliments. I did not know how to take compliments. The next day Nancy called Mrs. Warren and made an appointment for us to meet. When we went into the modeling agency, I looked around in awe. Chandeliers hung from the ceiling, royal blue carpet graced the floor and lots of gold and white decor enchanted the environment. Mrs. Warren greeted us and escorted us to her office. A woman came in and served Tea in pretty cups as Mrs. Warren explained in detail the possible career I could have, if Nancy allowed me to be signed up as her client.

I listened in disbelief thinking I was dreaming. There were pictures on the wall of famous models I had seen in magazines. The next thing I knew Nancy was signing on the dotted line. Mrs. Warren gave me a schedule for training classes and a photography session. Nancy sternly stated, "NO nudies... Rebecca Marie is a decent young lady."

Mrs. Warren assured Nancy that I would only do high fashion modeling. On the drive home, Nancy went on and on about the money I was going to make and how famous WE would be. I drove and listened without a word as reality set in, *How the hell can I model? I am going to let myself be the center of attention. Who the hell wants to look at me when there are so many pretty girls to choose from?*

Over the next four months, Nancy allowed me to use her car to go to Modeling class. I took lots of different kinds of training, failing in nearly every course. The photographer said I was not photogenic; my facial features were uneven thereby creating limits to the angles to photograph me.

In the "spoke persons" class an attempt was made to teach me to sell products. Well, I was so nervous that my stuttering returned. I would speak too low or too loud. It was hard for me to hold a smile and when they pushed hard for me to perform tears came to my eyes.

I took walking classes, which sounds easy but it was a challenge. Mrs. Warren wanted to train me to do the catwalk. The problem was my height because I was just too short at five foot seven inches. Nevertheless, she was determined and gave me six-inch high heels to give me height. Now I had to walk with a specific stride, hold my head up and let my head lead the way, my head turned first then my body followed. After weeks of practice, I finally had a success. My first show was a charity show of which many famous and important people would attend.

The stakes were high, if I did well at this

show, they would send me to New York. I was to model eveningwear... my favorite. They me fitted for sleek elegant gowns and we rehearsed until everything was timed perfectly. Nancy attended this show, dressed her in finest holding an elegant glass of champagne pretending that she was part of the elite crowd that bid on the high-priced clothing.

I waited backstage, my hair done in a giant up-do, my make-up done to perfection. I looked in the mirror and could not believe it was my reflection. I wanted to cry but did not dare ruin my makeup. The signal given and there I stood in front of hundreds of people. I walked out reciting in my head, each turn and each time I was to pose and then continue down the catwalk. I nearly held my breath and made it through without a glitch thinking, *Thank goodness, I didn't trip and fall.*

Once back stage, I was rushed into the next gown. Then hurried back to my waiting spot where a security-guard, complete with gun held a chinchilla coat for me to put on. I loved this part. The coat cost more than Nancy's house. When, the signal was given, I walked down the catwalk feeling like the Queen of England. I paused, posed and made my turn perfectly. At the end of the catwalk as rehearsed, I turned my back to the audience and let the coat slide slowly down my arms revealing the backless gown I wore. When the coat reached my hands, I walked away dragging the expensive coat on the floor and causing the audience to clap loudly. Just before I was to walk off stage I turned and took notice the people were giving me a standing ovation. I smiled and exited. Back stage

Mrs. Warren hugged me and I got congratulations from all the girls. Mrs. Warren told me, "You are too short for this industry but you were great and you can count on going to New York. Baby, you've done it and are headed for fame and fortune." Well, hell's bells, I let the tears roll out between my false eyelashes smearing my makeup. I finally did something right.

Later at the banquet, I received many congratulations from the designer and many of the people present. Nancy was on cloud nine to be hob-knobbing with the upper crust of society. Three weeks later, Nancy drilled me, "I will call you every night to be sure you are in early. Remember, I do not want you acting like a slut just because I am not there to keep an eye on you. Every Friday, you pay your hotel bill and send me the rest of your money. I have bills to pay you know. But I'll be sure to put some aside for your savings account."

I nodded not even really giving any thought as to how much money I was going to make. Off I flew, all by myself in a 747 plane to New York City! I was in disbelief thinking I was dreaming. When the plane landed, a man was holding a sign with my name. I went up to him and identified myself. He collected my baggage and drove me to the Martha Washington Hotel for Women in

Manhattan.

Many of the models stayed at this hotel. We were all very young and so this made it safer for us. I was in New York for a short time, a place where I would grow up really fast. I was incredibly naive. An innocent in every sense of the word and was brought up on the fear of god. I would go on calls every day and then I sent out to a job for a designer.

Although, I was not a photography style model the designers took pictures for their archives and advertisements. To my dismay I began to lose jobs really fast, some designers and photographers were gay and so I was safe with them except for the rude insults that was typical for the business, such as; You are too fat... too skinny, ugly, dark, pale, unsightly, stupid etc. With the straight men, photographers mostly, they propositioned me suggesting sexual favors and if I refused they would dismiss me and then report to the designer that I was unacceptable. Needless to say, I was not called back.

By the end of the third month, no one would hire me. The girls at the hotel told me it was not so bad, a night with the right guy will make my career. Well, I just could not do it. It was wrong and so I was on my way back home a loser, defeated and hating to disappoint Nancy.

Nancy was beside herself, furious as she ranted and raved. The jobs I did in New York helped her bank quite a lot of money. I'd get on average $1200 per show. She scolded me and called me a loser and no good for nothing. I never told her why I lost work thereby that too became another secret. She called the modeling agency and got Mrs. Warren to get me a few jobs locally but I was washed-up. I then got a job as a seamstress, it was union work and so it paid well. My Daddy was pleased to hear I quit modeling. I guess he understood about life, men and an innocent like me.

I only saw my Daddy once a year now. When we went for lunch there was not really much to say. I guess he did not know how to entertain me now that I was an adult. We still fed the ducks but what little we had of a relationship was dry now. I regret that I never attempted to talk to him. I often think about him and can't help being curious about how he spent his life.

At nineteen years old, I accepted I would work, give my check to Nancy and then eventually die. I did try to join the Navy as a last desperate attempt to amount to something but failed the physical. Nothing seemed to work for me. Life was empty and pointless for me. I was a drone plain and simple. All I had was my dreams, my fantasy of a man who would love me unconditionally. He would not care what I looked like or how stupid and clumsy I was; he would love me just as I am. My journals at this time became more of a wish list realizng none of it would ever come true.

Chapter 12

Lured by Evil!

I will pause here for a moment to say, abused children grow up to become abusers or set themselves up to be on going victims. Either way, unhappiness and downheartedness will consume their lives. Keep in mind that fate is in each person's hands; everyone has a choice and can overcome the statistics.

At nineteen years old, I felt starved for love and attention. I never dated and certainly never even kissed a boy. I could only dream what it could be like. I would watch movies, read books and ponder the day that my prince charming would come to rescue me. I did realize that my daydreams were false hopes but I had to have something to cling to, something that would give me a hope for a future of children, love and security. I did have men approach me on occasion but shy and mistrusting I refused them all. My time in New York taught me men could not be trusted. Possibly, there was a man out there destined for me but he would have to prove his worth, my virtue would not easily be given away. It had to be for love and only love.

Nancy and Louie never married but lived together like husband and wife. He would go to work and support the house and she did what she loved to do, she cleaned house, cooked and went shopping. She never missed church and dressed up like Jacqueline Kennedy, with her cute pillbox hat, gloves and purse with matching shoes even though that look had gone out of style. I never went to church because I had my weekend job and that was fine with me. My heart was no longer in prayer, God or church feeling that god never had a heart for me.

Louie was a nice man and endured constant insults and complaints from Nancy. The more time they lived together, the more she found fault in him. I have to admit feeling sorry for Louie at times. She was verbally brutal to him when she felt he did not give her enough money or when he was too tired and did not want to go out dancing. Another one of Nancy's joys was to ballroom dance. Louie was patient and pretty much let her bully him.

I watched and listened but kept my opinion to myself. At times, I felt like a ghost in the house, I came and went from job to job unnoticed for the most part. Except when, Louie's friend Tony came to visit. He was thirty-two years old and going through his second divorce. For the most part, I never spoke to him, only returning a friendly hello in passing. I often noticed him staring at me and sometimes he winked at me. I disregarded him thinking he was just being nice to me... because I was there.

One day Nancy was not home and Louie and his friends were sitting out in the patio drinking beer and just visiting. I parked the car in the back and so I had to walk through the patio to get into the house. I noticed how Tony watched me and I have to admit, it frightened me a little. I went into the kitchen to fix myself a snack when Tony entered.

"Excuse me. I just came in to use the restroom."

I nodded and tended to the making of my sandwich without a verbal reply. A couple of minutes later he walked up to me and asked, "Rebecca, would you like to go for dinner and a movie with me?"

Stunned, I nearly gasped, "No... you are a married man. My mother would never approve."

Tony took hold of my hand, "I am divorced. I am not married anymore. It's only dinner and a movie I want."

I felt the impulse to run, but calmly refused his offer and hurried out of the kitchen leaving him standing there. My heart pounded as I wondered if I should tell Nancy what Tony said. On second thought, I decided to forget about it, because Nancy would only blame me for acting like a slut.

A few weeks went by and I forgot all about Tony and his forwardness until he returned. He boldly gave me compliments on my appearance but was always careful not to say anything to me or about me in Nancy's presence. Tony visited Louie without fail, every weekend and would be sure to stay until I got home from work. He flirted with me constantly and I must admit I began to like the attention. I would blush, smile and offer a shy thank you for his compliment. It felt good to be noticed. I wasn't really attracted to him, he was short, and his face wasn't attractive, and of course, he was much older than me. I did not care for the fact that he was always drinking even though, I had taken to secretly drinking quite a bit myself. I never got drunk, no one ever knew about my secret bad habit.

After a few months, Tony began talking to me more, telling me funny jokes to make me laugh and persistently asking me out on a date. Yes, I fell for it. I felt flattered and enjoyed the attention. I finally told him, "You have to ask my mother permission if you want to take me out to dinner and a movie."

Tony smiled, like the cat that caught the canary and in fact hurried and asked for Nancy's permission of which, she went into a rage. Screaming and yelling at him, calling him a dirty no-good-for-nothing Mexican and forbidding him to return to her house. I was listening from my bedroom having an idea that this was exactly how she would react.

Nancy hated Hispanic people for some reason unknown to me. Louie tried to calm her down but once she was on fire there was no calming her. After Tony left, Nancy went into my room ranting and raving. I tried to explain that I did and said nothing to encourage Tony but she slapped me and called me a dirty slut.

The following weekend Louie and Nancy were back on speaking terms and he took her out of town for a big dance. They would be home the same night but very late. I made myself a snack and sat to watch TV after they left when I heard the doorbell. I ran to answer it and there stood Tony, "Let's go, it's early and I can get you back by midnight. Your mother won't be home till nearly dawn."

I of course greatly protested and insisted that he leave but he was persistent and promised to have me home early. I know it was foolish but I agreed. I ran and got my sweater and purse and made him promise to have me home by eleven o'clock. We drove off and I have to say it was very exciting. This was my first date and I anticipated a kiss, anxious to know what it would be like. This was not the man of my dreams of that I was certain. I thought that dinner, a movie and a goodnight kiss would be so much fun, after all that is how they did it in the movies.

We drove to a pizza place whereupon Tony ordered a pizza to go. I thought we would go to a restaurant but I did not want to complain, maybe he could not afford a restaurant so I kept silent about it. Then, we went to a drive-in theater instead of the Cinema like I expected, but, what difference did it really make, we were still going to watch a movie and again I assumed he might not be able to afford more than the lower price of the drive-in.

At the driven-in, we parked and enjoyed the pizza. I cannot for the life of me, remember what the movie was about or the name of it. We watched the previews of coming attractions and spoke a little about movies we liked. Conversation was to a minimum because I really did not have much to say.

When the movie finally started, Tony excused himself to go get us cokes and popcorn. I watched the movie while he was gone. Upon his return, he opened the trunk to the car and then approached the driver's side door with arm full of stuff. I reached over and opened the door for him. Tony suggested before he got in the car that we would be more comfortable in the back seat.

The car had bucket seats in the front but a bench seat in the back. I blushed thinking he was trying to set up an opportunity to kiss me. Well, what the hell, I was curious as to what it felt like to kiss. I quickly got into the back seat. I saw no wrong in a simple kiss. In the back seat, Tony had two empty cups and he asked me to hold them. He filled both cups with beer and this is where my protests began. I flatly said, "I don't drink. I'll just have a Coke Cola."

However, Tony said, "It's just one beer to wash down the pizza. Just one, don't worry."

Well, I did not want to ruin the night and my

secret truth was I handled alcohol very well. I was a closet drinker and managed never to draw suspicion or get caught. One beer would not be a big deal. I took a couple of sips when Tony pulled out a whiskey bottle and said with a chuckle, "I can tell you are not a beer drinker. Beer drinkers don't sip it. I got an idea... to make it taste better. Take a shot, real fast then chug the beer. It's good, try it."

I shrugged my shoulder, took the shot glass of whisky and quickly downed it, something I often did with tequila. Then, Tony pushed my cup as a signal to drink the beer fast. I did it and thought, it still tasted bad but it didn't seem like a big deal. I had another shot and another as Tony kept encouraging me.

I want to remind you, I was a strong drinker, often having four or five shots of tequila before work or school without losing a hint of my faculty. It was not unusual for me to enjoy three or four cups of wine without feeling a buzz.

What happened next changed my life, forever. I do not remember how many drinks I had but suddenly I had the strangest feeling. I could hear Tony talking and even-though he was right next to me it seemed like his voice was coming from far away. It was like, I was in a dream that I could not wake up from. I remember struggling, trying to push him away from me. My voice did not sound like my own... I know I was greatly protesting as he laid me back on the seat and was now on top of me. I guess I was making a lot of noise when suddenly everything faded to black. He had struck me and I guess knocked me unconscious. Of course, I have no memory of what else may have happened in that car.

The next thing I remember, Tony was lifting me out of the car. I think I verbally protested I could not seem to keep my thoughts straight. All of a sudden, he dropped me on a bed. I looked up in a daze and saw him taking his clothes off. I panicked but could not seem to control myself to stand or even sit up. I do remember trying to fight him off and I know he was hitting me but strangely, I felt no pain, none at all.

I woke from the sound of water running. I looked from side to side and did not recognize my surroundings. I lifted my head that ached terribly and took notice that not only was I nude but covered in my vomit. I sat up and could see that my legs and the bed were covered in dry blood. The smell was putrid and I felt sick to my stomach. My mouth was dry like cotton and my body ached, something awful. The bathroom door opened and Tony stepped out, naked and laughed, “Next time I won’t feed you first, look at the mess you made.”

Shocked and frightened I grabbed the dirty sheet to cover myself and ran into the bathroom. Tears flooded my eyes both from the physical pain and from the humiliation and the realization that he RAPED me! Crying I got into the shower and tried to wash away the great sin that was committed, scrubbing hard to clean my soul of the evil.

After I turned the water off Tony shouted, “Hurry up and get dressed so I can take you home.”

Home... Oh my god, Nancy will certainly kill me. I stayed out all night long ... what am I going to do? Should I call the police? My thoughts were racing as I tried to figure out what I could do to correct my situation.

Tony opened the bathroom door and tossed my clothes at me. “GET DRESSED!”

He shut the door and I scrambled to put my clothes on which were torn and badly wrinkled. Crying uncontrollably, I felt so frightened. I walked out of the bathroom and angrily said, “I’ll tell the police...”

Big mistake! Tony grabbed me by my neck and pushed me up against the wall. “I didn’t make you come with me; you came with me of your own free will. You got drunk because you wanted to... I didn’t make you drink. You got in the back seat with me like a little slut and got what you deserved. If you didn’t want to end up in bed with me then you should have stayed home. Do you think the cops will arrest me after they find out you voluntarily went out with me and got drunk. Try to make trouble for me and I swear I’ll kill you and don’t think I can’t do it... I have killed people for much less."

Frightened, I trembled ... he was right the whole event was my fault. I brought it on myself. I did act like a slut and I got what I deserved. I looked at Tony's angry face and believed he would indeed kill me if I went to the police. He made me promise not to go to the police or tell Nancy what happened. Fearing for my life and realizing how stupid I had been, I agreed. Nancy will no doubt beat me and I guess it's a punishment I truly deserved this time. I used washcloths from the bathroom to stop the flow of blood, never had my period been so strong. Then, I realized it was not my period but the fact that my hymen had been broke. I lost my virtue to a pig of a man. Now, no worthwhile man would ever want me. I ruined what little chance I had for a good future.

Tony drove me home and when he stopped in front of Nancy's house, he warned me again about trying to get him in trouble. He pulled a gun from the glove compartment and swore he would kill me if I said anything. As I got out of the car, he sped off and there stood Nancy at the door, looking at me from head to toe in disgust. I was a sight, unraveled, smelling of vomit, bruised and feeling the washcloth between my legs filling with blood. I hung my head as I approached Nancy waiting for the worst.

"You dirty little slut. I warned you, didn't I...? I told you that I didn't want you listening to that man!" Nancy furiously slapped me across the face and told me to go bathe and pray for my soul. I went to my room for pajamas when Louie demanded, "Did Tony force you to go with him? Did he get you drunk... did he make you drink..."

I interrupted, "No, he didn't force me. Tony invited me to dinner and a movie and I agreed. We did drink but he didn't force me... it was my choice."

Louie looked at me from head to toe, "Why did he beat you up... you are a mess?"

Looking down at myself and knowing I had to get to the bathroom immediately before I bled on the floor I said, "There is no one to blame but me. I'm fine."

That was that, I took a shower trying so hard to wash the filth and the sin off myself then I got dressed feeling beyond exhaustion. Just before I lay down Nancy entered my room, "He fucked you didn't he? Then, he beat you to make you do nasty things... right? He mistreated you because it was god's way of punishing you for not waiting to get married first. You stupid idiot... the only thing you had to offer a worthwhile man was your virginity. I should beat the shit out of you... but what's the use now? You make me sick."

With that, Nancy left the room and I sat there sobbing. She was right I was a stupid idiot. I was so worthless she did not even bother to beat me. I picked-up my MoMo, hugged him to my heart and went to bed. I slept nearly the whole day undisturbed. When I woke up, I wrote in my journal then went back to sleep. I was drained and disgusted and a bit confused, *how and why did I get so drunk? I had been drinking for years and never got drunk. It was so weird that I lost control to such an extent. Well, it will never happen again. I hate men, all men! There was one man out there somewhere looking for me, my prince charming but now he would not want a filthy slut like me. Idiot! Idiot!*

Chapter 13

No life of my own

Deeply depressed, I returned to regular routines. Work helped keep me busy allowing me not to dwell on the stupid thing I did. After a few weeks, I resolved to live my life for work, sleep and wait for death. I thought of all the possible futures I could have had and felt all was lost to me, no hope of happiness and worst of all, no hope for love.

I was now twenty years old and I had nothing to show for my life. I was nothing more than a drone working to give Nancy money. I felt so alone, Eddie-boy left me long ago and I had no friends talk too. In my whole life, I only had one friend, Judy. She was always nice to me and would sit and have lunch with me at school. However, she was dead now having died from some kind of lung disease. I needed someone to hold me, to comfort me and let me cry on their shoulder. I did not even have god to pray to anymore.

I want to take a pause here to explain to those readers who are thinking, "*That Bastard should be in jail. It was rape plain and simple.*" Well, this was a very different time. There was no such thing as date rape laws. I do believe that if I went to the police, after hearing that I went with Tony of my own free will, then proceeded to get in the back seat with him by my choice then willingly took the drinks... well, as awful as it sounds the case would have been dismissed. The results of my date from hell was legally my fault. Thank goodness that today, Date Rape laws are in effect and counseling for the victims are readily available.

Nancy did not allow Tony on her property but that did not stop him from driving up and visiting with Louie from the curb. On a few occasions when I came home from work, I would see him talking with Louie. Tony had the nerve to wink at me and flirt with me. I would hurry into the house terrified of him. I often had nightmares of him chasing me or trying to kill me.

A couple of months after my rape, I began to feel very sick. The smell of food would send me running to the bathroom to vomit. Every morning without fail, I was puking my guts up and then spent the day at work wishing I could just lie down and go to sleep. I spent about three weeks feeling depressed and could not hold food down. I did not tell Nancy because well, it was not unusual for me to be sick to my stomach. My Daddy called me and it was so good to hear his voice. He said he wanted to see me. Well, I wanted to see him. No matter that, he was an absent father most of the time; I needed someone who appeared to care. He agreed to visit me within a month or so because he was out of town. A month... well, of course I would have to wait.

I went to the doctor on a regular follow up. I still battled side affects of malnutrition and therefore went to the doctor often. I told Dr. Miriam, "My upset stomach has returned. I can't eat and even the smell of food makes me want to puke. It's worst in the morning but fades throughout the afternoon."

"Rebecca when was your last period," asked Dr. Miriam?

Thinking for a minute I replied, "I don't know. I am so irregular it's hard to remember. You know I often skip months."

She asked me lots of questions and then simply said, "I want to do a vaginal examine."

Shocked I gasped, "What for? It's my stomach that..."

"Rebecca, I think you might be pregnant."

My jaw dropped in surprise. I felt my heart pick up a beat as I felt nearly like fainting. After the examination and blood work, I got dressed and went into Dr. Miriam's office where she said, "You are pregnant Rebecca... are you engaged to the boy? What are your plans?"

I was utterly dumfounded. I did not know what to say or how to react. I felt like I was dreaming. Dr. Miriam gave me a prescription for iron pills and some other vitamins. I cannot even remember what she said to me.

As I walked home, I felt lifeless, in disbelief. When I got near the park, I sat on a bench and just let the news ferment in my mind. I watched kids playing on the swings and some adults playing tennis. I thought of my past then of the present and how I would deal with the future as a smile came to my face. *A baby! My baby to hold and to love. My child who will love me unconditionally.*

Joyful thoughts raced through my mind, of how I would spend my time with my baby. I would love him and treat him with kindness and understanding. Despite his conception, it was the happiness day of my life. I went to a store and looked at the baby clothes feeling like life could not be better. I went home and upon entering the house my thoughts turned to how I would live now. Nancy was sure to kick me out of her house. How would I support myself and get an apartment? Now fear overwhelmed me as I wondered how I could take care of a baby, keep a job and do what was right by my child. I felt so helpless and stupid.

Nancy looked at me, "What the hell is wrong with you. You didn't get fired did you?"

"No, I didn't get fired. I have a problem and I don't know what to do." I paused wondering how I could find the right words. "Well, get on with it!" shouted Nancy.

Keeping my eyes focused on the floor, I said just above a whisper, "I'm pregnant."

There was a long pause but I dare not look up at Nancy. She turned to quoting the bible and the terrible sin I created. Now I would have a bastard child and god would see to a just punishment. She went on and on as I wept. Then, she caught my full attention when she said, "you have to get married."

"Married? To who?" I gasped through tears.

Nancy narrowed her eyes, "How stupid can you be? You'll marry Tony of course. He is going to take responsibility for you and his bastard child. Do you think I am going to make it my responsibility? I am not going to devote my life to taking care of you and your brat!"

She stormed out of the room as I cried into my pillow. I was so afraid of Tony and now she expected me to live with him as his wife. Could things get any worse? I had no life of my own.

Nancy immediately got on the phone and called Tony. I stayed in my room holding my MoMo and fearing what the future held for me. It was not a half hour before Nancy came into my room and told me Tony was coming over. I said nothing and did nothing. When Tony arrived, Nancy summoned me into the living room where surprisingly he was happy with the news. Saying he would be responsible for his son and do the right thing. I did not love this man and he did not love me, he understood this but went on and on about the son he was going to have. I sat like a dumbfounded fool, I had nothing to say, no protests came from my mouth. This was my fate, I was sentenced and tried and now would face my lifelong punishment.

Nancy insisted that Tony pay for all the wedding arrangements of which he offered no protest. She gave him permission to visit me but forbidden to take me out on dates. Nancy went into high gear with this ridiculous wedding, it was not mine to enjoy or to plan but Nancy's to wholeheartedly enjoy. A big church wedding was in the works as I sat solemn and alone. Tony insisted that I quit my job and between the two of them, my life was theirs to control.

You are probably thinking, "*Say NO! Just go out on your own.*" However, I had no will of my own, having a strict catholic belief of right and wrong. My whole life was to bow down to submission and take the blame for all the wrongdoing. I simply accepted my fate. My only hope for a degree of happiness was my baby, who no matter what would be mine to love and protect. For him, I would endure any punishment and any amount of suffering because all that mattered to me was my baby's well-being.

I should have called my Daddy and told him but as always he put me aside forgetting that he was going to visit me a month after our last conversation. Months had passed and no word came, so I did not bother to tell him what my situation was, not realizing that this time he just might have came to my rescue. I guess I will never know.

Nancy dragged me to bridal shops in search of the perfect dress. I was a mannequin plain and simple of which she could live out her dreams. There was no time for lots of bridesmaids and such because I had to get married quickly to be sure no one would suspect I was pregnant. Tony came often to sit and watch TV with me, drinking beer after beer as usual. For the most part, I had nothing to say to him but I did notice that he was polite and respectful. We sat like to mindless puppets watching TV, me wishing he would leave and he ... well, I could only imagine what he was thinking about.

I still had not informed my Daddy of my upcoming nuptials. I just could not bring myself to tell him. Feeling miserable, I could no longer enjoy my nightcaps. I was pregnant after all and I would do nothing that might cause my precious baby any harm. In fact, I went on a quest for perfect health. The weeks slipped by quickly and now it was only two days until my wedding day. I thought of running away, but where would I go, what would I do? This was an insane situation, I was about to marry the man who raped me, beat me and humiliated me. How can it be and why was I so powerless to stop it?

All was ready for the day of my sentencing. That is how I felt, I committed a crime, Nancy was my judge and jury and Tony was my life sentence. I went to the store on errand. Taking my time, I browsed the aisles in the store trying to distract myself from what lay ahead in my life. An hour later, I returned home. Surprised, I found Nancy crying. It was a very rare occasion to see Nancy cry.

"What happened? Why are you crying?"

She wiped her tears, "Your Aunt Louisa just called me... your father died."

I stood dumbfounded; I had no real emotions to express. It did not seem to be real. I had no words to say and I did not know how to react. I simply walked to my bedroom and held my MoMo. *He's not dead... how can it be? It's a mistake. Why on earth would Nancy be crying if it were true, she never gave a shit about my daddy. Is this a dream?*

Nancy came into my bedroom and said, "You are his only daughter and so we need to go and make the arrangements for him. Whatever money or property he might have your Aunt Louisa is sure to try to get. You need to claim what is rightfully yours. You will have to postpone your wedding. You and I will try to contact everyone and tell them what happened, call Tony first."

I did as directed, still in utter disbelief. I did not shed a tear and I felt ... numb... nothing. We stayed up late that night and contacted as many people as we could. Some were unreachable so if they showed up for the wedding Tony would be there to inform them of the change in plans.

The next day, I got to see my beloved Aunt Louisa. I only was able to see her twice in my life but I always had such fond memories of her. However, this new memory of her would be drastically different. As I approached her, she shrieked at me, "You have to pay all your father's expenses! I cannot afford it! I had to be in charge when you could not be reached... you are his daughter it's your responsibility!"

Stunned, I could not believe such an angry bitter tone now came from this woman. How can it be, again I was dumbfound. I did not know what to say. I did not have and never had control of my money and now I turned to Nancy who snapped back at Aunt Louisa like a dragon. I stood there listing to the ugly exchange of words thinking, *if my daddy is really dead then how can they be fighting over money? Doesn't either of them have any heart? Could this be the same Aunt Louisa who was so nice to me?*

Suddenly, a man who approached stopped the arguing. He was a cousin who spoke in Spanish. I do not know what he said but it calmed my Aunt. She then said to me, "We need to go to the funeral home. Since there was no one else to make the decision I picked the funeral home for his body to be sent too."

I agreed still finding it unbelievable that my

Daddy was dead and in a funeral home. Strangely, I did not think to ask how he died. As we were about to get into Aunt Louisa's car, a car pulled up behind us and two men dressed in suits stepped out. They identified themselves as homicide police. My heart felt like it hit the ground, could it be that my father was murdered? In Aunt Louisa's house, Det. Flannigan told us how my father died.

"Your father's body is still in the hospital and will undergo an autopsy. His death raises questions. According to my report, he was at a friend's house, a regular routine of poker night. He got drunk, too drunk to drive home and slept on the couch. When his friend tried to wake him up for work, Mr. Mendez was dead. Mr. Mendez showed no sign of illness and in fact worked the day of his poker night. A sudden death with no explanation is always suspicious therefore we need to investigation and find the true cause of death."

Aunt Louisa said, "I was told he had a heart attack."

Det. Flannigan replied, "Yes, it appears as a heart attack but the autopsy will verify it or tell us a different story."

I sat and listened, no tears, no emotions thinking, *My god, is he really dead? I don't believe for a moment that any one murdered my daddy. My head aches... I wish I could go to sleep... I need peace and quiet.*

After Det. Flannigan asked his stream of

questions about my father's lifestyle, he left and by now, my headache made me feel nearly lightheaded. I said nothing as we decided to go to the funeral home to make the arrangements. At the funeral home, the funeral director went on and on about music, flowers, and church services. I felt like I was dreaming and everyone's voice sounded like muffled into background gibberish. I sat there like a wooden doll wondering when this craziness would end.

Suddenly, the funeral director handed me a glass of water, "Are you all right?"

I looked up at him and simply nodded but welcomed the glass of water.

"Miss Mendez, I have a nice selection of coffins for you to choose from. Please, follow me."

COFFINS! My god he wants me to pick out a coffin... I can't breath... I need air...

"Excuse me; I need to go to the rest room." I said in a desperate attempt to escape.

"Through this door and just past the first chapel is the ladies room. We'll wait here for you," said the funeral director.

I hurried to the bathroom and put some cold water on my face. I took some deep breaths and felt if I did not lie down and rest I would just pass out. *I'm fine, I'm fine... I'll hurry and get this whole thing over with then we can leave.*

I selected a steel-blue coffin with matching lining and decided on a navy blue suit for my father to wear. Once they delivered the body to the funeral home, we would be notified. The ride home seemed to take forever. Once home I was relieved and attempted to hurry to my bedroom for some much needed rest when Nancy shouted, “Wait a minute.”

I turned and she continued, “I don’t have the money to pay for your father’s funeral. What are you going to do about it?”

“But, since I was with the modeling agency you have been banking a savings for me. Surely there is enough money in all this time to pay for...”

Nancy interrupted, “You think you can live here for free? You use water, electricity, food and... well, I pay for all your expenses. You are an adult now and so I used your savings to cover your room and board.”

Stunned, I just stood there for a moment thinking the funeral director said it would cost over four thousand dollars for all the arrangements. Where on earth would I get that money? This was just too much, I was on the breaking point when Louie suggested, “Get a loan and then you can make monthly payments.”

Nancy was pleased with that solution and said I was to find a finance company to take the loan out in my name. Tears now came to my eyes not because my Daddy was dead or because I didn’t have a penny to my name and never got to enjoy any of my earnings. Tears came to my eyes because I simply emotionally over the edge. I went to my room and curled up under the covers with my MoMo whereupon I cried myself to sleep.

The next day we went to Avco Finance where I took out a five thousand dollar loan. It would take five days to process it before I would get a check.

On the third day, my daddy arrived at the funeral home. Cause of death, I don't remember the technical words but he died from an enlarged heart due to heavy alcohol consumption, high blood pressure and so on. He was not murdered, but died of natural causes.

On the day the check arrived, I went to the funeral home to pay the bills. This was the first time I saw my Daddy's body. I was alone and glad of it. I walked into the chapel and there he lay in the coffin I picked out for him dressed in his navy blue suit. When I touch his face, a rush came over me, reality set in as I looked upon my dead Daddy. So much went unsaid between us and I never told him I loved him. I never told him I was about to get married and have his grandson. It was all too late. He was gone.

I sat in the first pew and cried for a long time. The funeral director came in and told me, "The rosary starts in a couple of hours, you should go home and get some rest."

I agreed and left for home but stopped at Lake Merritt first to feed the ducks one last time. Emotion now overwhelmed me and my tears seemed to be uncontrollable. At the rosary that night, I did not even hear the praying, I just stared at my Daddy wishing he and I could have been closer. My thoughts filled with things I wanted to tell him and things I wish he had told me. I thought of my baby who would never know a grandfather and felt life was so unfair.

Chapter 14

Greed, Betrayal and Punishment

The size of the funeral surprised the traffic police as well as the funeral director and me because thousands of people arrived for the service. The large church filled to the max and so a second service held to allow the crowd that waited outside to share service too.

I was astounded that my Daddy knew so many people. The Mendez family was indeed large to boot. My father's Military buddies show up and hundreds of Longshoremen stood proud to honor my Daddy. Men from the pubs that my father frequented wore T-Shirts identifying from which establishment they were from and brought huge wreaths.

Flowers surrounded My Daddy's coffin, so much so that the priest decided to place them throughout the church as more and more flowers arrived. My Daddy was greatly loved and all these people knew him better than I did. How is it that our relationship was so distant and so empty when he was a man with so many friends who loved him?

I felt cheated not to really know him and a

bit jealous that he preferred the company of all these people to me. Then, cousins came up to me and asked with a tone of anger, "So what do you think of your father's death... do you even care?"

My jaw dropped, why would they ask me such a thing? Of course, I cared but I was not a person who knew how to express emotion and so they took my silence in the wrong way. I found out that most of the Mendez family did not like me, thinking that I along with Nancy turned our backs on my Daddy. My god, how could they blame me for what happened between my parents?

Next came the long, long process to the cemetery. The funeral directed called in extra motorcycle cops to direct traffic. My goodness it was like a dignitary died. A smile came to my face as pride filled my heart. I believe my Daddy must have been a very wonderful man. So many people came to show their respect. How different I was from my Daddy because I did not even have one single friend. Again, how I wish I could have known my Daddy better.

It was a military service complete with a twenty-one gun salute. My father had been a war hero having earned two purple hearts. When the soldiers began to fold the flag, as the bugle played it was a truly emotional moment and yes, I cried. The soldiers offered the flag to my Aunt Louisa who pointed me out, as his daughter. I could tell Nancy got upset thinking she was the widow and should receive the flag. Oh yes, Nancy now played the part of the grieving widow despite that she and my Daddy had been divorced since I was four years old.

After the service at the gravesite, we all walked toward the cars when a man came up to me. "Hello Miss Mendez. I represent the Longshoremen insurance. Your father did not name a beneficiary so I came to see who would receive the flag. Here's my card, please come to my office tomorrow so we can talk about your inheritance."

I just nodded not really paying attention. In the limousine Nancy snatched the card from my hand whereupon Aunt Louisa angrily snapped, "I get half! I was the one who was here for him when he needed..."

"You were his sister of course you were there for him but Rebecca Marie and I need that money," hissed Nancy.

I just sat quietly and listed to the two of them argue over who gets the money. I did not care and I would not say one word about the money. I greatly believed in ghosts feeling that both Eddie-boy and Grady may have been ghosts. If my father's spirit was watching I did not want to say or do anything that would make him think bad of me, it was only money after all.

I watched Nancy and my Aunt in disgust, the greed was amazing. I have to say it really surprised me to hear my Aunt Louisa act in such a way, I thought she was... so different.

The immediate family totaled over hundred people, my father had eight brothers and four sisters who all had children and grandchildren. It was the largest family gathering I had ever seen and this was just the immediate family. As with most funerals the usual program of food and talk of the diseased filled the rest of the afternoon at my Aunt Louisa's house.

I wanted so desperately to leave, I was not feeling well and I was so tired, it was all I could do to keep my eyes open. It was beyond me why Nancy wanted to stay and visit with this family that she hated so much. Finally, when we got up to leave my Uncles were very gracious as each wished me well. Even though promises to visit each other were expressed, we all knew this would be the last time I would ever see any of them.

Out by the car my Aunt Louisa reminded me that she was to get half of the life insurance. I made no reply as the car drove off. If it were up to me, I would simply give her the whole amount. I really didn't care.

Nancy interrupted my thoughts, "I retrieved your father's wallet and check book. I also ordered lots of Death Certificates; we are not going to be saddled with his bills. Tomorrow that money grubbing Aunt of yours is going to meet us at the bank. Your father had an account and most likely had a nice sum of money tucked away. You'll be married soon so you won't need it. I agreed that I would split half with that bitch Louisa. But we need you to sign the papers." I nodded wishing that I could simply shout, "Shut up!" but of course I sat silent wondering when it would all end and I could just sleep.

That night I slept so deeply that I do not even remember dreaming. Yet, I did not feel any better when I woke up. Tony wanted to know when the wedding would be. Nancy as usual answered for me, "We have to wait a month, Rebecca Marie is in mourning and it's disrespectful to have a celebration right after a funeral."

The date was again set. I realized I would be four months pregnant by the time I got married. Nancy was so concerned that people did not find out that I was pregnant yet; my baby would be born only five months after I was married. The truth is I didn't give a damn at this point I. didn't care what people thought.

At the bank, I signed the papers and stepped aside to let Nancy and Aunt Louisa get their cut. They reminded me of hungry wolves fighting over the kill. There was quite a lot of money to divide between them. Then my mother claimed my Daddy's car. I gave no protest not wanting to be part of their greed.

Upon leaving the bank Aunt Louisa sternly said, "When you get the life insurance check I get half... remember half!"

Nancy glared at her before we turned and

left for the car. On the drive home, Nancy went on and on about something or other, I do not remember a word she said.

The insurance agent informed me that it could take up to ninety days before I received the insurance check. The truth is now that I thought about it; I wish I could pay off the loan with some of that money. I was wondering how I would pay the loan back after Tony insisted I quit my job. He had this crazy idea that I would cheat on him if I were in the job force or socialized. I felt like a puppet with no will of my own.

My wedding day, felt like my heart broke. I was not happy; I was not in love and looking to a bright future. Only my baby kept me going, the hopes of holding my precious baby and loving him is what gave me purpose.

Our wedding-night would be considered by most a joke. Tony got so drunk that he passed out to my great relief. We had a studio apartment so there was no privacy, no other room for me to go to for escape. I sat in the dark trying not to make any noise for fear that I would wake him up. The thought of him touching me or wanting sex made me cringe in horror. At dawn, he got up without a word, took a shower and said, “I have things to do. I’ll be back home early.”

“There is no food in the refrigerator. What am I...?”

Tony gave me a ten-dollar bill and said, "Right next to the apartment complex is a burger place. Get your food and then eat it here."

After he shut the door I thought, *this should be a day of bliss, I should be in love with my new husband. He should shower me with terms of endearment and not want to leave my side. Instead, I am glad to see him go. Maybe he will get in an accident and I will be free.* I sighed to have such thoughts and went back to bed as I held my MoMo.

Tony did not come home that night; it was well after dawn when he called. "I need you to come pick me up. I can't find my keys."

"How can I pick you up? I don't know where the keys to your truck are kept."

Tony replied, "They are inside my shaving kit in the bathroom."

He told me where he was and I drove there, finding him in an ally behind a house, standing next to his car. He did not appear to see me so I honked the horn. Whereupon, a lady came out of the house, and she ran up to me and said, "Here are Tony's keys; he was so drunk last night I was afraid to let him drive home. Now don't misunderstand Tony and I are only friends."

Tony walked over, took the keys from me and ordered me to go home, which I did. I was so stupid at the time; I thought the lady was only a friend. My god, the man cheated on me after only a day of marriage. But what the hell, she did me a favor by keeping him away from home.

When Tony returned home that night, he was drunk and my nightmare began. I was now free of Nancy but at the mercy of Tony. He was brutal with me as I learned the truth about his sick ideas of lovemaking. He felt that if a woman enjoyed sex, she could not be trusted. Well, he knew I had no experience and so he began to teach me what my role would be as his wife. He liked resistance, he wanted to see me scared and in tears. He could not get an erection until I was trying to flee for my life. He did not really hit me but shoved me and pushed me, when he put his hands around my throat threatening to kill me I shouted, "please... the baby... don't hurt me!"

With that, he let me go and I ran for the door, this is what he wanted to see. I was in a panic, fearful for my life and the well-being of my baby. He yanked me by my hair and shoved me over to the bed where he actually raped me. I was fighting, kicking and struggling as he penetrated me, roughly and brutally. This was a horrible assault on me, thankfully he ejaculated almost immediately.

Tony shoved me aside and proceeded to simply go to bed. I ran to the bathroom shaking and sobbing deeply concerned that he may have hurt my baby. All that night I stayed as quite as a mouse so as not to wake the monster who now dominated me.

After he left for work the next morning, I went to the bus stop. I had health insurance and a few dollars and so I went to the doctor. My thighs and arms were bruised a little but the doctor did not make any comment about it. I asked if sex could harm my baby. To my dismay he replied, "Not at all, your baby is floating in fluid. You can have sex until you are ready to deliver. Don't be concerned about it."

After the prenatal check-up, I caught the bus back for home. I felt devastated to think that I could not tell Tony that sex would harm the baby. Strangely, he did want the child and said he had to claim his son. For some reason we both knew it would be a boy, there was no doubt.

My life turned into a new kind of hell. Nancy was horrible to me as she beat me and starved me, but now I had to endure sexual abused and I was not emotionally ready to accept it. I would watch movies and read books and sex where was described so beautifully. I came to realize lovemaking was only a fairy tale, another one of God's jokes on women.

What was I to do? Well, my solution for every impossible situation was to slip into my own fantasy world. I would tell myself, *he'll change when the baby is born. He'll see that I am a good wife and that we have a beautiful baby together. He'll then begin to care about me and possibly become a loving father and husband.* This was how I began to deal with every aspect of my life. I would plan a future of happiness with this horrible man I married, knowing full well, he'd never change. Nevertheless, my fantasy helped me get through the day.

Transportation became a constant problem. Tony did not want me to go to the doctor or the store without him; he mistrusted me to such an extreme that it became ridiculous. He would call during the day just to be sure I was home. He would not take time off work to give me a ride to the doctor or the grocery store. What was I to do? I finally said, "This is not working, I have to go to the doctor and I need to buy groceries."

"You want to go out and get fucked don't you?" grunted Tony with an evil glare.

Shocked, I replied, "I would never do such a thing! Never! How can you say that?"

I convinced him to let me use the car but he made rules. I had to prove I went to the doctor. He allowed me to go to the grocery store but not take more than an hour and I had to go in the mornings only. Well, even Nancy would not have laid out such rules. I was a prisoner!

His drunkenness overwhelmed me at times with fear. He would talk about killing me as he cleaned his guns. "Killing you would not even be an effort. Nobody in your family cares about you and you have no friends. I could bury you out in a field and nobody would even ask what happen to you. Cheat on me or try to leave and you are as good as dead."

There I sat with a swollen belly, thinking, *What the hell is your problem? Where would I go in this condition? I hate you... I hate you!*

Early the next morning, I checked the mail and held the largest check I had ever seen in my whole life. My Daddy's life insurance had arrived. All kinds of thoughts of how I would like to spend the money came to mind, possibly a savings for my baby or a new car for me. Maybe even a divorce and freedom in which to rear my baby and live out my life happy. However, I knew I had to give half to Nancy and the other half to my Aunt Louisa. I was thinking of asking them if they could just spare me a little to pay off my loan.

When Tony came home, I showed him the check and explained I had to give it to my aunt and mother. He chuckled as he snatched the check from me. "Neither one of those bitches are going to get a penny of this check. First, I will pay off your loan then the rest of the money is for me to decide how it is spent."

I began to protest but Tony took on that evil look as he shouted, "What's yours is mine! I'll talk to your aunt and mother."

Well, I do not know how my aunt took the news and to this day, I have never seen or heard from her again. As for Nancy, denying her that money destroyed what little relationship we had as she became even more bitter toward me as time went on. She never really said anything to me about the money but I felt her anger when she looked at Tony. She had every reason to hate him I did agree to give her the money after all.

When I was into the later part of my seventh month, we moved to a bigger apartment, two bedrooms and a living room. This was nice, I had more space to separate myself from my husband. I happily fixed up a nursery for my baby and tried to make the apartment a nice home.

As the days wore on Tony's drinking got way out of control. Often, he would tell me about the other women he slept with and how I disgusted him. He said he hated fat women and I now looked like an ugly cow. My god, I was pregnant what did he expect I would look like?

Seven weeks before my baby was due, Tony arrived home in a rage with his hand bloody with scraped knuckles. He got into a fight at the bar. He went to sleep almost immediately from drunkenness. I sighed in relief.

During the night as I slept, I suddenly felt hands around my neck. Tony was straddling me, "Where is he? Where is he hiding? I'll kill him then you!"

I gasped as I felt his hand tighten around my neck, "I don't know what you are talking about. There is no one else here."

He jumped off me and picked up his gun than ran to the closet, shouting, "Get out of there!"

Of course, no one was in the closet. He ran through the apartment looking for a man I supposedly was hiding. My god what a nut! After a few minutes, I think he understood that he had been dreaming or something. He ordered, “Go to sleep!”

Tony went back to bed and I lay there afraid to move. I believe he had been dreaming and woke confusing reality with his dreams. If I had reacted poorly like screaming or something, I am sure he would have killed me. I wanted to pray to god but knew he would not hear my prayers. I quietly cried myself to sleep.

When I woke the next morning, the day met me with another brutal rape. Tony left for work as I heaved great tears feeling that I would not be able to endure this constant punishment. I went to take a shower and to my horror, I noticed blood running down my leg. I quickly got dressed feeling my backache. I called the doctor and explained what was happening and he told me that it was very early, but it sounded like I started contractions. He said it was nothing to worry about just to get some rest and keep him posted.

I lay on the couch feeling my backache terribly and feeling deeply concerned about the spotting (bleeding). I called the nurse two times and gave her my vitals and again she told it was nothing to worry about. Tony always went to the bar after work so he did not get home until about 10 p.m. stinking drunk. He started to push me around but I snapped, “I’m bleeding... please, I think the baby might be coming!”

He looked at me for a moment then just went to bed without another word. I was up all night, as the pain grew worse. Just before dawn, I went to wake up Tony so he could take me to the hospital, but he was still in a drunken stupor and would not wake up. I got dressed packed my bag for the hospital and was about to drive myself when the worst agonizing pain surged through my spine.

Crying, I could hardly breathe. Finally, he woke up and grunted, “What’s wrong with you?”

“The baby is coming...I need to get to the hospital...now!”

He rolled his eyes and causally got dressed then drove me to the hospital. He stopped the car at the front entrance with the motor still running and said, “Okay, you’re here. I’ll be back to pick you up when it’s time for you to come home.”

My jaw dropped, he was actually just going to drop me off at the door. I hated him more than ever now. I got out and walked into the hospital where I checked myself in and a nurse took me to the maternity ward. I went through thirty-six long hours of hard labor. I arrived on Friday and Josh was not born until Sunday morning.

There was a problem with the delivery and Josh literary torn his way out. I needed lots of stitches and was in distress. My baby was premature but doing fine. He was large for being premature, weighing in at five pounds three ounces and so only needed twenty-four hours in the incubator. I was in the hospital for two days after Josh was born and in all that time, Tony never called. I did call Nancy the day Josh was born and told her I had a boy. She did not seem to care.

The lady I shared the hospital room with had a stream of family visiting her and filling the room with flowers. Hopefully, she understood how lucky she was to have a whole family care so much about her. I was not jealous of her but it made me feel so alone. I had no one to come and see my precious little baby. He was mine to enjoy alone. I held him and fed him so overjoyed to finally see him, grateful that he was healthy.

The day I was to go home, the nurse called Tony to pick me up. I have to admit he seemed genuinely happy to see our baby boy. Later that day Tony told me that if I had delivered a baby girl he would have dumped me like trash. The bastard actually thought he was doing me a favor. No matter, all I cared about was my precious baby boy.

Chapter 15

All Mine To Love

Up until this point in my life, I always turned to my MoMo for comfort even as an adult. Now, my heartfelt filled with love for my son. Josh was my comfort, my salvation and my happiness. I put MoMo away into a trunk for safekeeping. Having had a very difficult delivery, needless to say, I was in pain. My vaginal muscles would not contract and so, Josh literary tore his way out of me. I was in distress during his delivery and Josh at one point was stuck in the Birth canal, unable to breathe. Josh was born small but normal and the Doctor told my recovery would take longer than usual.

Tony wasted no time with me or Josh, and quickly left to be with his friends. This was fine with me. I needed help with a new born but preferred to tackle this new responsibility on my own than to have Tony stay home and torment me.

Well, I was in a real pickle because I had no experience what-so-ever in caring for a newborn infant. I had cloth diapers because disposable diapers were a very new item and not commonly used as they are today. I for the life of me could not fold the diaper small enough to fit Josh's tiny bottom. Frustrated I got the scissors and cut the diapers down to size. I guess it was rather funny not realizing the importance of why diapers need to be thick. What a mess I had within minutes. Every task was a struggle. My poor baby was so fragile as I tended to the business of bathing, feeding and caring for the love of my life. After lots of trial and error, things became easier as my days filled with the care of my precious little baby.

However, when Tony came home my smile faded as I hurried to make dinner while trying to keep Josh from crying. He cried a lot and Tony blamed me for not knowing how to take care him. One particular day when Tony came home good and drunk, I just could not stop Josh from crying. I fed him, changed him and cuddled him in my arms but he continued to cry.

Tony growled at me to keep him quiet, "Can't you even take care of your own baby? Quite him up I am trying to think! Where's dinner!"

I picked-up Josh and held him in one arm as I hurried to serve Tony a dinner plate. Josh wailed something awful. I served Tony his dinner. He looked at the plate then threw it against the wall making a terrible mess and causing Josh to cry even louder.

"Put the baby in his room... then come here," he hissed at me.

I hurried and placed Josh in the crib and turned on his mobile that played nursery rhymes. He cooed a little as he watched the mobile play. I hurried off to the living room knowing I was in for some trouble. Tony grabbed me by my shoulders and shook me hard. I felt like a rag doll with my head going from front to back out of my control. Then, he shoved me to the couch as he glared at me. He grabbed my arm again and squeezed extremely hard then knocked me to the floor. He did not really hit me but shoved me and squeeze my arms causing dark red welts. Josh started crying again and Tony's face went pale with anger as he shouted, "You stupid bitch, you can't even take care of my son!"

Tony kicked me on my left thigh and knocked me on the coffee table and to the floor. I laid there in a panic listening to Josh scream out. I thought that maybe Tony would hurt my baby to quite him, but instead he turned to me.

"I should kill your worthless ass..." With that, Tony began undoing his belt and zipper. I stood and ran toward Josh's room. Tony grabbed me by my hair and smacked the side of my head against the wall. Then, still holding on to my hair he yanked me to the bedroom where he pushed me back on the bed.

"Please, I am not healed yet... the doctor told me to wait...."

Tony did not care about me or what the doctor said as he tore off my clothes. I put up protest whereupon he forced himself on me, penetrating me as I struggled for escape. He was done within seconds although it seemed like an eternity to me. He rolled off me and then he simply went to sleep. I grabbed my robe, ran to Josh's room and picked him up. Feeling my body ache as tears flowed from my eyes. I stayed that night in the living room and slept with Josh in my arms. Tony got up early as usual and simple left for work.

This was my marriage, my new life. By day, I was a happy mother and by night, I was only a thing for Tony to abuse and treat worst than an animal.

I began to see that Tony did not intend to hurt his son and in his own way actually loved his son. He did not hold Josh or bond with him because he believed his role as father was simply to provide. I also began to realize that he just wanted to humiliate me, to make me feel worthless and his idea of marital sex was only for his pleasure or procreation.

Tony repeatedly told me when I tried to make protest about how we had sex, that only a slut who cannot be trusted enjoys sex. A wife simply services her man and tends to the house and kids. Hell's bells, where did this man come from to have such stupid ideas? True I had no experience but from the movies I watched and books I read the marriage bed was something of beauty where two people made love and did not simply have sex.

What could I do to change my situation? In that day and age, it was NOT a crime for a husband to rape his wife. I had no one to go to for help and I was afraid of being on my own not knowing how to provide for my baby. Worst, Tony continuously threatened me with death if I ever tried to leave him. He would say, "Try to leave and I'll find you, catch you and cut you to pieces then bury the pieces all over the desert. No one will ever know what happened to you and then I'll take Josh away and my family will help me raise him.".

The stories I heard of his ignorant backwards family, made me shudder in fear should my poor baby be placed in their hands. All that mattered was Josh, my life was only as important as my baby's need for me. I would put up with Tony tormenting me and ensure my baby's well being.

Within six month, Tony talked about buying a house and the plans were in the works. I was happy with this and began thinking; *He'll change when we get a house. He'll have too much obligations to be getting drunk and pushing me around. Josh is getting bigger and so Tony will learn to be a good and caring father and husband.* And so, went my constant need to fantasize for a better future, knowing down deep inside that he would never change.

It was not long before I began to realize that Tony was into serious criminal activities with bad men. For the most part, he kept his companions and his dirty dealings away from me. Yet, I could not help but to overhear phone conversations and mysterious late night deliveries. On occasions, as I was doing my general cleaning, I found drugs, in little bags. Although, I had never taken drugs I did watch a lot of movies and so I recognized narcotics when I saw them. I did not know what kind of drug they were but I was not completely stupid. When I confronted him on it, he went into a rage shoving me and pushing me around then he threatened me with death.

This is when things became more intense to say the least. Now, he began pointing guns at me and often held a gun to my head as he raped me. My fear became so alarming that sleep became a struggle. I was nervous and concerned that he would in fact kill me. My only concern was for my baby, who needed me. I pretended not to notice what Tony was up to and turned a disinterested cheek in hopes that he would back off. I asked no questions and simply tended to my tasks. Nevertheless, Tony feared that I might know too much and turn him in. I did not really know this man, or what he was up too and I knew nearly nothing about his past.

Then, Thomas, Tony's kid brother who was only a teenager came to visit us. Thomas was a pleasant sort, nothing like Tony. We would spend afternoons talking about his family and Tony's past. Well, I got an ear full as I began to learn about this brutal man, who was not only wanted in his country for felonies but was a murderer to boot. Thomas told me of bloody family feuds between his brother and neighbors in Mexico. Tony grew up on a ranch, illiterate and ignorant and was taught that the strongest survive and that women were simply property to carry on the next generation.

Thomas being very young was not involved in any of Tony's criminal activities from the past or the present. When he realized that his older brother was into dealing drugs and taking drugs, Thomas went back home to complete his education. Now I looked upon Tony realizing I had to play his game or suffer dire consequences.

I endured Tony's need to dominate me and torture me, and insomnia set into such an extent that I always felt weak, exhausted and depressed. I did not realize how depressed I was as I wore a fake smile for my son, always trying to spare him the horrors I had to endure. He was a little boy and I was determined to make his life a happy one of love, no matter what was going on behind closed doors.

I was a victim of abuse but put on a show of happiness as I explained away bruises with, "I fell. I bumped my arm cleaning and so on. Those early years of marriage I was sent to the hospital several times with injuries and just like I did when I was a child, I lied to the doctors by saying I fell. I knew that no one would come to my rescue after all, no one ever saved me from Nancy when I grew up no matter that I nearly died. This was my life and I accepted it. Deep in my heart, hatred and anger festered as I paced my living room at night unable to sleep.

Yet, happiness filled my heart because Josh was all mine to love. My baby, my purpose and for him I would face the devil and burn in hell to ensure his well-being.

Chapter 16

Me, Josh and Baby makes three.

A year later, we were living in a nice house with a large fireplace and a beautiful front yard and back yard. The world saw Tony and me as a happily married couple with an adorable toddler. No one knew what happened behind closed doors. Even my precious son, was naive to my late night torment.

On a few occasions while Tony was roughing me up to rape me, Josh woke up to the noise. Tony never wanted anyone to know how we lived or how he treated me. It now became the task of hiding my sexual abuse from our son, who was only in the next room.

Tony pushed and shoved me, knocking me to the floor as I endure his sexual abuse in complete silence. No one can imagine what is like to endure such punishment in silence, without a moan ... without letting out the noise of sobbing. My torment intensified and I worked hard to be quiet for my son's sake. Tony was his father and I would do my best to let Josh think that his father was a normal hard-working man and I was just clumsy and thereby often bruised.

This was one of my biggest mistakes. I hid

my suffering and in doing so, Tony took on the look of a caring father and husband, thereby who would ever believe me if I suddenly told the truth. I was sealing my fate and letting Tony take complete control of my life. I became a drone again and had no freedom, no friends and no social life.

I could not be out after dark and had to prove where I went and why. If I took more than a couple of hours, Tony would actually go look for me, thinking he would catch me with another man.

Meals had to be served on time even if Tony was not home. He often came home late and there was no telling when he would be on time. I was only twenty-two years old but I felt tried and old and wanted desperately to have a complete night's sleep. I returned to my nightly shots of tequila for a degree of comfort. I was a heavy drinker sneaking two and three bottles of tequila a week into the house and hiding it in the laundry hamper. I was good at my secret drinking, I was never drunk and always in control. Tony never suspected which always brought me back to how I got so drunk that night he took me to the movies.

Well, my question was answered one Saturday afternoon as I washed the dishes. The kitchen window overlooked the front driveway where Tony and a few friends drank beer and talked. One of the guys asked Tony, "So do you have the stuff? There is a beautiful young girl I know but she won't give me the time of day. You said, the stuff will make a woman do whatever you want and she won't even remember the next day. How much for the stuff?"

Tony replied, "I'll give it to you for fifty dollars."

I stood on my toes, looked out the window and saw Tony hand over a small packet as the man gave him the fifty dollars. Then Tony said, "Put it in whisky or beer so she won't taste it. It works pretty fast and you only need to put a little in the drink."

The anger in me nearly made my blood boil. The bastard drugged me that night then took advantage of me. He ruined my life just to have sex. If it were not for Josh, I would kill him. The dirty bastard! I looked over at Josh playing with his trucks and signed in bewilderment. It did not matter what Tony had done, it was done and a drug had sealed my fate. Then, I thought of the poor innocent girl that would fall to the same fate and there was nothing I could do to help her. Why was god so cruel to women, why did he allow such things to happen?

*****

Watching Josh at play, one day, I felt sorry that he was so alone. There were no other children or people for that matter in his life only me and of course his father who paid him no attention at all. Watching Josh, I thought he needed a little sister or brother to be his companion in life, so he would not ever be alone. When Josh and his sibling were grown and married their children would be cousins and their families would have what I missed in my childhood. I thought about it and then stopped taking my birth control pills. I wanted another baby, if I had to endure Tony molesting me then I at least wanted another baby to love and share his life with Josh.

I went to the doctor who warned me that having another baby was risky. "Your delivery was very traumatic. You lost a lot of blood and Josh could have easily died. A second pregnancy could be worse," explained the Doctor.

I insisted, "I want one more baby and then I'll have my tubes tied."

"Well, if you have made up your mind then we'll need to follow a regular routine of vitamins and rest, it's better for the baby if you can carry him full term. We'll plan to have a caesarean section and not let you go into labor. I expect you to come in every three weeks till you deliver," explained the doctor.

I nodded and gathered all the paper work vowing to follow all the doctor's orders. I was so excited wondering if I would have a boy or a girl. I began planning and getting ready even though, I was not pregnant yet.

However, disappointment turned to depression as a year then two passed and I still had not gotten pregnant. Josh was four years old now and as cute as he could be. He was not only my son but my companion and friend. I enjoyed taking care of him, reading him stories and watching cartoons with him. During this time I learned to deal with Tony on his terms, sex was a nightmare of anger and brutality but when he got a new girlfriend, he would leave me alone. Yes, he enjoyed the company of other women and was sure to tell me when he was drunk just how much better those women were from me. What an ass-hole. I did not care what he thought about me and I was grateful for his short-term girlfriends for allowing me some peace from him. His relationships never lasted more than a few weeks or a couple of months at most.

As soon as I gave up on the idea of ever getting pregnant, you guessed it; I got pregnant and was thrilled to the point of tears. Josh and I went and purchased baby clothes and a few toys for the new member of the family. I bought a cute little teddy bear for Josh, my way of giving him some comfort that he would never feel pushed aside for his new sibling.

Then, fear took over when I got so ill that I could not eat a single bite of food without vomiting. This was worse than the morning sickness I experienced with Josh. Fear gripped me that I might lose the baby. The doctor kept assuring me everything was fine. Yet, I lost eighteen pounds in my first trimester. It was a difficult time to say the least. Being so ill and having to fight off Tony was no easy task as depression consumed me. But like the switch of a light, I woke one morning feeling fine and it was all behind me. Within a few weeks, I was the picture of health as my pregnancy proceeded. Josh was so cute as he happily helped me fix his room for his new sibling telling me he would help me take care of the new baby. "It's my job," he would say with such pride and a sense of responsibility.

I made it into my ninth month and, two days before Josh's fifth birthday, I had to go to the hospital to deliver. I hired a nice lady, Dina, from an agency to take care of Josh for five days while I was in the hospital. I felt so bad not to be with Josh for his birthday. I delivered a healthy baby-boy, whom, I named, Mitchell James. I phoned Josh on his birthday and said, "Happy birthday Josh, guess what I got you?" After a pause I said, "You have a new baby brother, his name is Mitchell." Josh started chattering away telling me that he was going to take good care of his brother and show him how to play with his Legos. I promised to be home soon.

Upon my arrival, Dina and Josh greeted me as they both ran out to the car to help me in. Tony was his usual cold self. He had dropped me off at the hospital and I did not see him again until it was time for me to go home. At the house, he simply turned on the TV and ignored us. Dina was kind and helped me get settled in bed. I had surgery after all and was in bad shape and a lot of pain. During the delivery the doctor, tide my tubes so I could not have any more children due to the high risk of serious and lethal complications in future pregnancies. I was so happy to be holding Mitchell and have Josh right next to me that I did not care about the future.

I had paid Dina for five days and now she had to leave. But I desperately needed help and no matter how much I pleaded, Tony refused to pay her a penny more. Nevertheless, Dina insisted on staying to help me for free. I was touched by her generous offer and when Tony was not looking, I gave her the money I had stashed in one of my shoes. I learned back when I was a child to always keep emergency money in the house. Neither I, nor my children would ever go hungry. It was only seventy-five dollars but I insisted that she take it and to please not mention it to Tony.

Dina stayed for another week and a half then she had to go due to another assignment. The week and a half was a wonderful time for me despite my discomfort. Tony did not want to go near me because of my surgery. He said, "Your stitches and scare make me sick. My god, you can't even have a baby the normal way. At least you had a boy, I swear if you brought a girl home I'd kill you both and take my son far away to a better place. You are nothing but a worthless bitch. I am going hunting with my friends. I need to get away from you... you make me sick!"

I looked at him as he started packing his

duffle bag and thought, *You asshole, I hope you get shot in the woods and never come back.*

Dina was wonderful as she tended to my every need. I made every effort to get back on my feet. What I really enjoyed was the talks I had with Dina. I never really had a friend so this sisterly bonding felt good. She taught me many things about tending to an infant and I enjoyed watching how much she liked Josh and read him a bedtime story every night.

After the kids were in bed Dina sat with me and said, "It's not my business but you need to get away from that son-of-a-bitch you are married too. He is mean and uncaring toward you. He never went to see you or the baby when you were in the hospital. He should be home with you but instead he goes off with his friends... I heard what he told you. How can you live with that man?"

I sighed as I replied, "What choice do have? He threatens to kill me and take my son off to be reared by his backwards ignorant family. I do not know how to take care of my children and maintain a job... I have no real skills. Now that we have a second baby, maybe Tony will come around and see the light. Maybe he'll change."

Dina looked at me for a moment then said, "Who are you trying to fool, me or yourself? If you were my daughter, I'd take you away from here. Just keep in mind you always have a choice."

The day Dina drove off, I felt near tears. She

was a good friend but she was now out of my life. I would make the best of my little family, which was me, Josh and baby makes three. I never recognized Tony as part of my family and he did not care in any event. He was a ghost in our home as he came home from work, ate, went to bed and often, very often punished me with a night of torment then left for work.

Once he came home from his hunting trip, he told me to sleep in the other room. "You make me sick. I can't believe you let them open up your body to have a baby. I don't like how you smell. I hate the feel of your hair on me. You are only good to fuck and take care of my kids... so get out of my bedroom!"

Although, I was grateful to have my own bedroom, it hurt me terribly to think I was seen as disgusting, unsightly and only good as his housekeeper. This pig of a man though I was disgusting! He never kissed me or embraced me, ever. He said kissing was nasty, yet he was the one with the rotten teeth and foul breath that polluted an entire room. I tried to take care of myself and my teeth, never wanting to offend people with my breath.

At night, as I lay in bed I dreamed of a man who would come to my rescue, he would love me and see me as beautiful, he'd kiss me all the time and appreciate me and respect me. We would be so much in love that life would be a never-ending honeymoon. My fanciful dreams helped me get by and my children were my purpose and my source of happiness.

Chapter 17

Evil Never Dies

I can imagine what you are thinking. What a fool I was to continue to live with such a cruel heartless man and have his children. Remember, that abused children often fall into the hands of an abuser. I believe that the abuser looks for a certain personality to dominate. If I had shown confidence and assertiveness from the beginning Tony would have never taken an interest in me.

Nancy conditioned me to believe that I was worthless and unable to take care of myself. Nancy enjoyed dominating me because it gave her a sense of power. I hated Tony, wished him dead and daydreamed of running away but, my children were more important than me. Tony provided for their every need. He was neglectful of his sons but he would never harm them. Again, this was an era where it was not a crime for a man to rape his wife. I knew it and so I fell into the stereotypical battered-wife syndrome. I walked on eggshells trying to do everything perfect. I lied about bruises by saying I was clumsy. The young women of today are so lucky to be so well educated and protected by law. Yet, I know there are still women like me suffering and even dying by the hands of their husband.

Josh was now in Kindergarten and I happily

took him to school in the morning and picked him up at noon. My children were my world and during the day, I was a happy housewife and mother. Little did I know just how far Tony's criminal activities would affect me.

I knew nothing of what he was doing with the exception of occasionally overhearing conversations over the phone. It began to frighten me just how much terror Tony and his companions caused in the underground community of drug activity. For my safety I cannot go into those details but will say that theft, abductions, torture and murder were happening, of which I knew some details. Tony realized it and now his threat of killing me became more intense.

"If you try to leave or speak to the cops, I'll kill you, butcher you and throw your remains for the animals to eat. I'll take Josh and Mitchell to my family to learn what it is to be a man. Don't push me.... I'll kill you!" His words echoed in my mind.

Now, the sexual abuse that I endure involved guns. I was terrified of dying and had no one to turn to for help. Tony would force intercourse on me while holding a loaded Gun to my head. I squeezed my eyes shut waiting for the bullet to enter my brain. Then, there were those nights when he was so drunk that he would use his gun as his tool of rape. Shoving it brutally into my vagina and often cutting me with it.

I remember, one night as he cleaned his gun

he kept glancing at me. I could hardly swallow, my mouth dry from fear. I put the kids to bed and heard Tony call me to his bedroom. Nearly trembling I went to the room where he met me with a fierce slap across my face. He shoved me to the bed and ordered me to just lay there. I watched him put the clip into his gun and take the safety off. I got up and ran for the door, but he caught me by my hair and hit me on the side of the head with his gun knocking me to the floor. I felt dazed for a moment before I noticed the blood running down my face. What was I to do?

I attempted escape but he overpowered me, and punched me in my face. Usually, he never hit me on my face but he was in a drunken rage. Sprawled on the floor he came over to me holding my head back with his left arm while he used his legs to spread my legs apart. Then, he forced the gun into my vagina and said, "I am tired of you... I can do better. You are a lousy fuck and so that is where I am going to shoot you until I empty my gun. Then, I'm taking my boys far away."

I felt adrenalin pulse through my body as I squirmed for escape. Then, Tony started a countdown and when he got to ten, he pulled the trigger. I gasped in terror but there was no bullet. He got up laughing thunderously, "You dumb bitch... When I kill you, you won't know when it's coming."

I got up and ran to my bedroom trembling

and sobbing trying to get control of myself. I had to leave, I had to get my sons and leave this mad man before it was too late. But how, he had control of all the money and I didn't know a living soul who would help me.

Then it happened, a hope for freedom. As I fixed dinner and fed my children, I was pleased Tony said he had his pool tournament to attend to and that he would have dinner at the bar. This put a smile on my face. This news meant he would not be home before 2 a.m. and therefore, I would have a nice evening with my children, and hopefully Tony would come home so drunk that he would just pass right out. Thomas was visiting us again in hopes of registering for school and getting an American education. Tony always made an attempt to control his behavior towards me in front of others, especially his family.

I watched TV while Thomas played with Josh and Mitchell. It was amazing how different Thomas was from Tony. After the kids were in bed Thomas and I sat to watch the news when the phone rang. I answer it and said hello.

"Tony was in a fight. I'll come pick you up and take you to the hospital," said the voice.

Well, Tony warned me never to listen to any such calls and to wait and hear from him first. Mistrusting I asked, "Who is this?" The voice replied, "I am Ed, Tony's friend. He got into a terrible fight and is in the hospital. Give me your address and I'll come pick you up."

That was the red flag, this man did not even know where we lived therefore he was not a friend of Tony. Tony surely would not send a man, even a friend late at night to pick me up. I replied, "What hospital is Tony in?" Ed replied "County general." I said, "I'll call and check then get there on my own power." Ed started to make protest but I hung up. I told Thomas what Ed said and he suggested that I call the hospital, which I did.

It was true Tony was in the hospital emergency room and the nurse said that he was seriously hurt and that I should come at once. I told Thomas and he suggested that I go to the hospital and that he would watch the kids. I grabbed my coat and purse and drove off to the hospital, thinking that Tony was an asshole and probably got his nose or an arm broken. I could not help but to think, *Good, I hope your injuries hurt like hell.*

When I entered the emergency room, it was filled with Tony's friends. A few had blood on their clothes. They all looked at me with frowns of concern. The nurse took me aside and said, "I need you to brace yourself. Sit here, the doctor wants to talk to you. I sat in a cubicle alone wondering what the hell happened. The doctor approached me with two policemen and two other men dressed in suits.

"I am sorry to tell you that your husband is in serious condition and is not expected to live. He was in a shoot-out at a bar. He was shot in the head, twice in the chest and twice to the abdomen. He also has a shotgun blast to his side that removed muscle. We are preparing him for surgery. We'll do all we can to save him," explained the Doctor.

Well, I was dumbfounded and I hate to say it but I felt rather relieved. It would all end now and my suffering would be over. One of the men said, "You don't' seem to be upset by this news. Are you all right?"

I simply nodded not knowing what to say. The doctor said, "Would you like to see your husband... this might be your last chance to talk to him."

Shocked I gasped, "He's conscious?"

The doctor replied, "Yes, he's conscious at the moment."

Well what the hell, with all those injuries and he can talk! I nodded and stood up as one of the police officers said, "We need to talk to you before you leave the hospital."

Again, I simply nodded and walked off with the doctor to see Tony. At the door, the nurse said, "You need to be strong. If you react poorly you'll scare him and we need to keep his heart beat stable."

I nodded and she opened the door. As I entered, my first reaction was to the putrid smell of blood. They had not cleaned up Tony yet and there was blood all over him. I took notice of a basin filled with bloody towels. The sight of so much blood and the smell was overwhelming. I suddenly could not take another step. I felt light-headed but the nurse took hold of my arm and whispered something to me. I could not hear any sound and everything seemed to slow down as if I was dreaming. Suddenly, Tony spoke, "Is Josh and Mitchell all right... are they here?"

I looked at Tony for a moment then replied, "They are home with Thomas."

Tony then said, "I am dying. Tell my boys that I was a good father and that I love them."

One of the attendants pulled a sopping wet towel from Tony's side exposing raw muscle, which caused my knees to buckle. Two nurses grabbed my arms and quickly escorted me back to the waiting room. The nurse gave me a drink of water and made smell what I thought was ammonia.

A man said, "I am Det. Dubois. I am sorry to disturb you at a time like this but I must ask you some questions."

The policemen mistook my state of mind as grieving over the probability that my husband was sure to die. Tony would get no grieving from me. I simply felt shaken to the core from the bloody sight that I was never going to forget. It was pure terror, the smell and the visual burned in my mind.

After what seemed like endless questioning, I had nothing to tell the police. There was no way I could have known how and why Tony was shot. I was told that Tony was not expected to make it through the night and that I should stay. I spent the night in the waiting room and called Thomas a couple of times to check on the kids and let him know Tony's condition.

At dawn, the doctor told me, "We can only wait and see. The trauma to his body is... well, he has two bullets in his heart cavity but they did not pierce his heart. We removed two bullets from his abdomen and cleaned the gun shot blast to his side, which will need skin grafting later. There is a bullet in his head, it entered at the base of his skull but did not pierce the bone or the brain. Instead, it seemed to travel around passed the ear canal and lodge under his left eye. There is a possibility he might be blind in that eye. At present, we cannot predict if he'll survive or not. Go home, get some rest and I'll keep you posted."

I signed as I walked to the car thinking, *I'm free. He'll be dead before long and I'll be free.* I began making plans on how I could support my kids and survive. I put the radio on and felt the weight of the world lifted from my shoulders. I knew it was cold and heartless of me to think like that but I simply did not care. I knew there was life insurance from his union and I could sell the house and bank that money. I would get a cheap apartment and maybe take in children to care for so I could be with my boys. My mind was racing as to how I would make it on my own. When I got home and told Thomas the news he of course felt bad for his brother but said to me, "This could be a new start for you. I hate to say it but my brother does not deserve you. I do not wish him dead but I have to admit he is a bad man. Rebecca, I can't help feeling sorry for you."

Thomas was a good soul, the polar opposite of his brother. He was very young but saw things clearly. I told him, "Well, I thank you for your sentiment and I want you to know if Tony does die you can stay on until I sell the house. Maybe you can help me with some of the bills."

Thomas nodded and played with Josh while I tended to Mitchell's needs. Although, Tony was never mean to Thomas and in fact very good to him, I could tell that Thomas did not really like him. I do not know the whole story but I think it was very difficult for Thomas to grow up in such a backwards ignorant family.

As the case unfolded, the police kept me informed. Apparently, it was a kidnapping gone wrong. Det. Dubois told me that a witness and two of the gunmen came forward with the truth. A woman, her name was Lily, a former hooker and intimate friend of Tony's set him up by calling him out to the parking lot of the bar where the pool tournament was taking place. Once outside, four gunmen confronted Tony and told him to to get into a car. When Tony refused, they pulled guns on him. One man standing the closest had a shotgun in hand aimed at Tony's mid-section. The plan was to tie him up then take him to an out-of-the-way place then call me. I was to take money to the location on the pretense that they would release Tony. Then, their plan was to kill both of us and take the money.

However, Tony surprised them knocking the shotgun out of the way, which fired and took out the muscle tissue to his left side. Tony went to the ground, pulled out his pistol and started firing back. He shot two of the men and the others got a way. During the gun battle, they shot Tony multiple times as he ran and ducked between parked cars. The two injured gunmen were dumped by their companions at the hospital entrance and then made their getaway.

The Detectives questioned me about Lily. I only remembered her from the time Tony called me to pick him up at her house the day after we got married. My god, to think there was a plot to kill both of us and leave my children orphaned. Det. Dubois told me, "If your husband survives I suggest that you divorce him and keep better company. He is no good and it's my guess he's into drug dealing that's why Lily and her companions tried to abduct him. They thought he had lots of money thereby feeling it was worth a kidnapping. Your husband is not an educated man or holds a high paying job. I spoke to his friends and from the look of them... well, you'd be better off without those people in your life."

I nodded in agreement and shook Det. Dubois hand. “Thank you. I will follow your advice.”

I spent every day at the hospital while Thomas babysat for me, waiting for Tony to die but he hung on. Within three weeks, they took him off life support and although in serious condition, it looked like he would pull through. His friends began visiting him at the hospital sneaking in beer and illegal drugs but it was apparent that nothing would kill Tony.

Seven weeks after he was shot, I drove him home from the hospital. His doctors were amazed and all congratulated his miraculous recovery. I became his caretaker, changing bandages and tending to his every need. We were constantly going to different doctors all who were amazed that he was recovering so well. Even though Tony still had health issues to deal with, he was back on his feet and out with his friends once again.

He was fully recovered within six months of his release from the hospital. He returned to being as mean as ever. Both Nancy and Tony, only appreciated me so long as I could nurse them back to health. I suppose because of that it became in my nature to want to take care of people in return for love.

Thomas told me, “Get out... you are a smart woman and can make it on your own. You need to get away from him and keep your boys safe. I am moving in with some friends. I can't live here... I have to go."

My life returned to one of torment and misery. But, I started hiding money and plotted how I would get away from this man. I had to leave... I had to try and make it on my own. I now feared for my life and that of my sons. I no longer let Josh take the bus to school after Tony warned me that another attempt at abduction might happen. He said it they would most likely go for me or the boys. As far as I knew Tony didn't really have any money to speak of, why would anyone want to take his family for ransom? When I tried to question Tony on the matter, I suffered the consequences and so just kept my mouth shut and planned how I would get away.

Chapter 18

Escape!

Faking that he was unable to work due to his injuries Tony and I went on welfare for a time. This gave him the freedom to go deeply into drug dealing. Tony began using heroin, at first sniffing it up his nose then later I began finding syringes. He would hide drugs in the house and continuously threatened me with death if I ever told anyone or spoke to the police. That summer, I only let the boys play in the backyard. I lived in fear of something happening to my boys or me. I had no one to turn to for help.

During this time Tony became such an addict that he lost all interest in sex, which I have to admit was a relief for me. However, he became very paranoid thinking I would turn him in. His brutality heightened to such an extent that I began sleeping with a knife under my pillow.

He came home one day looking rather unraveled, I asked no questions and tended to my children. I was in the kitchen with my boys when I heard the doorbell ring. Tony opened the door and I heard two or three voices talking in low tones. Curious and needing to know what to expect, I stepped closer and listened in on the conversation. I didn't know who Tony was talking to so I'll say voice one or voice two to identify who spoke.

Tony asked, "Is he dead?"

Voice one, replied, "No, the bastard won't die. We did as you said and stuck the ice pick in both his ears, really deep. I stabbed him too. He's still alive!"

Voice two, said, "I shot him twice but didn't dare shoot him again or the neighbors might call the cops. I hit him repeatedly with a hammer ... to his head. This morning I could hear him moaning. My garage is a mess, blood and shit everywhere. We need to get rid of him!"

Tony replied, "Dead or not we'll bury him and be done with it. Then, we need to go after his wife, she is sure to call the police to report him missing. I never liked the bitch and I got this idea she might suspect that we did something to him."

Voice number two asked, "I worry about your wife. What have you told her... what does she know?"

Tony replied, "The stupid bitch doesn't know anything and I won't let her know anything. You have nothing to worry about."

My heart pounded in fear, they had turned to torture and murder and now plotted the death of an innocent woman just because they thought she might call the cops. I had to get away, before it was too late. The next day I went to visit Nancy, something I often did now in hopes of getting in her good graces. She was mean to me and scolded me about anything she could think about, my appearance, my marriage, how I dressed my boys and so on… She often expressed pity for Josh and Mitchell to be stuck with Tony and me as their parents. Nevertheless, I was tolerant of her scornful words and tried hard to create a sense of family. I was in desperate need of someone to turn to but it was obvious Nancy was the wrong person to go to with my worries.

One afternoon, after I put my boys down for a nap... all hell broke out. I sat in the living room with a cup of tea and turned the television on. When suddenly, from the back kitchen door and through the front door policemen dressed in black with dogs stormed in. One of the policemen shouted at me not to move. "Who else is in the house!" he shouted.

Rather stunned I gasped, "Just my children, napping." Then I took notice of a large dog running toward the boy's room. I stood up in a panic knowing the dog would scare Josh. But the policeman knocked me to the floor shouting something or other; all I could hear was Josh's screams then Mitchell wailing out in terror. I shouted, "Please, you are scaring my children!"

Suddenly, the policeman yanked to my feet and shoved over toward the couch. One of the police officers identified himself as Officer Denton, then handed me a warrant to search the premises. At that moment, Josh and Mitchell ran to me. I held them up on my lap trying to comfort them.

Officer Denton said, "Keep your arms around your children and I won't handcuff you. While my men search your home, I want to ask you some questions. First of all, who are you, is this your home or are you visiting?"

Shaken to the core as I held my children I replied, "My name is Rebecca, this is my home. Why are you here, what is happening?"

Officer Denton then asked, "We have had your home under surveillance for a few weeks and I don't remember seeing you coming or going. I never saw these children either. Have you just moved in? Is Tony your husband or boyfriend?"

I replied, "This is my home and Tony is my husband since 1975, why are you here?"

Officer Denton then explained in detail how he has been watching Tony and a few of his companions, traffic drugs. He said he came to find drugs and arrest Tony. "I don't want to arrest you. I don't think you have anything to do with all this mess. If there are drugs in the house tell me or we'll tear the house apart, the furniture will be destroyed and even the carpet lifted to find what we are looking for."

Feeling near tears I replied, "I don't know anything about Tony's drug dealings. He tells me nothing."

One of the other police officers came out of the master bedroom carrying rifles and pistols and proceeded to set them out on the living room floor. After three trips to the bedroom to bring out all the guns Officer Denton asked me, "Do you have permits or paper work on these guns?"

I shook my head and replied, "No, those are Tony's guns and I know nothing about them."

Suddenly a voice shouted out, "Eureka! I found the stash. The officer came out carrying a small suitcase and opened it in front of me. It was filled with small bags of narcotics, I assume heroin.

"What's your story? I found this under the baby's crib... don't tell me you know nothing about it." Spat the Police officer.

Officer Denton then said, "I am sorry but this changes everything and I will have to arrest you for position of illegal narcotics and an alarming amount guns which are probably illegal too."

The feeling of dream state came over me, all the noise seemed muffled, as I looked at all the chaos going on, my home was being torn apart. I held my children confused and afraid. *Jail... my god... they are going to take me to jail! How can it be? I have never done anything wrong.*

My sons and I sat in the back of a police car and taken to the police department. My boys were put in the care of a social worker while I was interrogated. I knew nothing about Tony's drug dealing, who his source was or from whom he sold it too. After a time, Det. Denton told me, "I don't believe you are guilty to any of Tony's crimes. I am sorry you have to arrest. Do you have any one who can come and pick up your children? If they are taken by social services they will be sent to Forster homes."

The thought of losing my sons made me heave great sobs as I pleaded with Det. Denton to show me some mercy. Nevertheless, a female police woman took me to a small cell and the boys sent to a place called Child Haven.

After a few hours, I was back in the interrogation room where a lawyer sat waiting for me. "Hello, I will be your lawyer, my name is David Myers. Det. Denton asked me to help you. Your brother in-law Thomas posted bail for you. You can go home ... with your boys in a couple of hours. The charges stand however and you and I will need to talk so I can prepare your case."

I nodded and thanked this wonderful man who came to my rescue. As I was about to walk out of the police department, Det. Denton came up to me and said, "I can see that you are a decent respectable woman. Take my advice and use this time to divorce your husband and go to a safe place. He'll go to jail for a long time and most likely get deported."

I shook Det. Denton's hand and thanked him. Thomas was waiting outside for me and together we went to pick up the boys. Thomas told me, "I used every penny I could get to bail you out of jail. I have to pay it back to some friends as soon as possible. Do you have any money?"

I nodded, "Yes, we'll go to the bank tomorrow."

When we arrived at the house, Thomas had to nearly kick the door in. The house was in shambles furniture torn up the carpet turned over and clothes, towels and garbage everywhere, making it hard to open the front door or the back door. I sat and cried thinking this was all too much to handle. Josh went up to me and said, "Don't cry mom. I'll help you clean up."

I looked at my little boy and felt so grateful to have him in my life. The next day I went to the bank and withdrew what was left of my inheritance. I gave it to Thomas, thanking him a million times for helping me. He immediately went back home having obligations to tend too.

I found out that Tony was arrested in a raid at his friend's house. They were caught in the act of packaging drugs. I thought this was good. I would sell everything and go far away. This was my chance to finally escape and start a life of my own. But as always, things were not as simple as they seemed. I had never been successful at running away.

I met with my lawyer Mr. Meyers, who was a public defender. I told him my story and then he shuffled through his papers. "There is no real evidence against you. Yes, drugs and guns were found in your home and you were the only adult in the house making you responsible at the time. But, your husband has taken all the blame, he will plead guilty and in return the police will drop any charges against you."

Surprised, I asked, "Tony took all the blame...willingly?"

Mr. Meyer replied, "From what I gathered Det. Denton had a talk with him... He told him that if you go to jail, you would lose both the children. The Boys would go to foster homes then go up for adoption. Therefore, to save your sons Tony agreed to plead guilty and save you from prison. Det. Denton may have crossed some lines but he is good at what he does. You don't deserve to go to prison, or lose your boys."

With a great sigh of relief, I thanked Mr. Meyers. "You'll still have to go to court and have your charges formally dismissed." said Mr. Meyers.

I shook his hand and thanked him again. Then, I went to the police station in search of Det. Denton where I shook his hand and thanked him for helping me. He repeated to me that I needed to get out of my marriage and take my boys to a safer better environment.

At home, I pulled out a map and wondered where I could go. I needed to go as far as I could get. I heard a knock at the door. I answered it surprised to see Yolanda, a neighbor who had always tried to make friends with me. She asked me how I was and told me she witnessed the day the house was raided. Yolanda sat and asked me what I was going to do now. I told her I was going to get as far away as I could and divorce Tony. She smiled and told me, "I am happy to hear that, I don't know what it has been like for you but I never liked him. Rebecca, I suggest you go to Las Vegas."

Shocked, I gasped, "Las Vegas? I can't go there I have children to raise and I need a job. That place is nothing but casinos and strippers."

Yolanda asked, "Have you ever been there?"

I shook my head and she continued, "It's a good place to live, it's cheap... I mean real cheap as far as rent and food. You'll find work there and don't worry you don't have to work in a casino. You'll really like it and find that it's easy to make a living there."

I thanked Yolanda for her suggestion and then began thinking that Tony would never think I went to Las Vegas. I'll never have to see him again."

I embarked on selling nearly everything in the house. When I went to court, I saw Tony dressed in an orange jumpsuit along with his friends. I sat quietly thinking that some people were so nice. Out in the corridor Det. Denton had a policewoman sit with Josh and Mitchell to watch them. I simply did not have anyone to leave my children with while I was in court. I listened to the charges against all the defendants and found it astounding that they pleaded not guilty. They were caught in the act after all. Tony however, stood up and pleaded guilty where upon he was taken back to jail to be sentenced at a later date. The charges were dismissed against me and I happily walked out of the courtroom.

A few weeks later, I went to Tony's sentencing to see what his situation would be. He looked at me but of course, we had no contact. I had the boys sitting next to me each with a book in their hand to keep them quite. After all the charges were repeated and a repetition of the guilty plea was stated, Tony was sentenced to five years in prison. I was free... free!

Within a couple of months, I drove to Las Vegas and secured a place for me and the boys to live. As Yolanda said, it was really cheap to live in Las Vegas, much cheaper than if I had stayed in California. I rented a trailer in a trailer park, it was a nice clean place with a swimming pool, play ground and walking distance to schools. The park was only a couple of years old so everything looked new and fresh.

I drove back home and rented a small U-Haul truck and packed it up. I went to Nancy's house and informed her of my decision. I told her how cheap it was to live in Las Vegas and after exploring the stores, market and even a restaurant, the prices were so low it was amazing. Well, at this point in time, Nancy was having some finance since she broke up with Louie and she took an interest in what I was telling her. She told me, "When I can afford it I might drive up and see Las Vegas for myself."

That pleased me, we had a nice talk, which was a rare thing for us and then I was off on my merry way. I put the radio on and gave Josh and Mitchell coloring books to keep them busy. We stopped in Barstow for lunch and drove around for a place to eat when I saw a McDonald set up in a train. Well, the boys shouted for me to stop there, which I did. It was so much fun, the drive and all the things we saw. When we arrived at our new home, I never felt so happy. This was MY home.

Chapter 19

Failed Again

The tiny trailer was adequate for a while, my goal was to buy a house and simply live in peace in my own home where I was in charge and nobody could mistreat me. I tried to spend the money I had rationally. I sold nearly everything in the house but the house went to the IRS for the most part due to Tony's drug dealing.

We lived simple but happy, my boys and me. However, after about six months, the money started thinning out and now I had to deal with getting a job and day care for my children. I had no real skills with the exception of being a seamstress but there was no such industry in Las Vegas. Day Care would cost me more than I could earn in a month. I became desperate wondering how I could survive and take care of my children.

When I did not make a month's rent, I went to the mobile park office and told them my situation and that I could work for them in exchange for rent and minimum wage. They agree to pay me minimum wage and I could keep Mitchell with me while Josh was in school. I still had to pay rent; there simply was not enough money to meet all our needs.

The local Catholic Church offered free well-baby check up and shots so I took the boys there to be sure they were healthy but food was a problem. I began to event crazy meals like Cheese cats, which was a hotdog bun with a slice of cheese. I found a special at the market; hotdog buns for a quarter and so I bought a bunch and put them in the freezer. I would toast them with butter for breakfast and make them like grilled cheese for lunch. The local casino buffets were really cheap. The Circus Circus was the only casino at the time where children were allowed. Dinner buffet was $1.99 per adult and half price for children and free for children under five. I would make Josh say he was nearly five and Mitchell was obviously a toddler so I took a big purse and we ate like pigs for a $1.99 then I'd stuff my purse with food and rationed it when we got home. I know it was wrong but I had to feed my kids. I just could not go to welfare, it was so humiliating and I kept telling myself that it would all work out.

The air conditioner broke in the middle of summer. It was 120 degrees and we lived in a trailer. I had the boys wear just underwear and I would spray them with water and give them popsicles to stay cool. A few times, we slept out in the car because it was cooler than in the house. When Fall came, the temperature was not so bad but Josh got really sick. I took him to the church and the nurse deeply concerned for Josh called a social worker so I could get Medicare for my boys. She was very nice and within a day, I took Josh to the doctor whereupon the doctor said Josh needed surgery because his entire sinuses were block and he could die from lack of oxygen to the brain.

Due to the emergency, the social worker expedited the paper work and the next day, Josh was in the hospital being prepared for surgery. Mitchell and I spent the day in the hospital waiting for Josh. The surgery was a success and Josh was allowed to go home. However, it was a long recovery and many other doctor visits. I thanked the nurse at the church and the social worker for helping me.

I juggled a job that paid $3.50 per hour, taking care of Josh while he was sick and tending to Mitchell. Much of the work I did, mostly typing and stuffing envelopes, I was able to do at home. I did some babysitting for the neighbors and even joined the PTA but try as I might to be a good provider and mother, I had to go hungry some nights to be sure my kids ate. I would cry into my pillow at night feeling like such a loser. Then, the car broke and I had no transportation. Everything was far from where I lived and public transportation was weak.

Nancy came to visit. She really wanted to see Las Vegas and possibly look for a home there, not liking to live in California any more. It was convenient for her to stay with me because it would be free. She went on her own exploring the town and called a Real Estate agent and within a few weeks actually found herself a nice house for dirt-cheap. Her house in California was on the market for $250,000 and the house she purchased in Las Vegas was only $55,000 this could give her a nice way to retire, not that she ever really worked in the first place.

Nancy saw I was struggling and food was limited but she offered me no help and I knew better than to ask. She went back to California to settle the sale of her house and returned a couple of months later with Sam and his family who were helping her move, all excited to be in Las Vegas. I was not involved and tended to my own life not having any real time to devote to them anyway.

When the boy's birthdays approached, I was so downhearted. Their birthdays were only two days apart and I didn't have any money to buy them a present. It didn't look like I would be able to complete the rent either. I watched my boys at play not having any idea that anything was wrong. I made them a cake for their birthday and tried to make the best of our situation. They were as happy as they could be and did not know any better than to expect presents.

When the first of the month came, I only had half the rent and by the 10th I owed late charges and then the first was upon me again. Finally, I received an eviction notice. I had nowhere to go and no one to turn too. I would be out on the street with my boys. I wanted to scream for help.

I sat in the living room writing in my journal and the boys were playing in their room when I heard footsteps go up to the front door. I felt my heart nearly stop thinking this was it, I was going to be kicked-out. A knock came and I just looked at the door afraid to open it. When the second knock came, I walked over, opened the door and stood speechless. It was Tony!

"Can I come in?" He asked.

I never got the divorce because I simply did not have the money. Now he was back, what was I going to do? Josh and Mitchell ran to see who arrived. Mitchell of course did not know Tony but Josh shyly said, "Hi dad."

Tony smiled as he looked at his sons, "They are so big... I missed them."

I told the boys to go back to their room and Tony sat on the couch. I sat in the opposite chair not knowing what to say, I wanted him to leave. I was so afraid. How did he find me?

"What do you want? How did you get out of Jail? I thought you were supposed to be there for five years." I asked.

"I got out in a year for good behavior. I want to apologize to you. A year in jail gave me a lot of time to think. I am sorry for... everything. Let me come back and I can take care of you and the boys. We'll get a nice house and I promise no more drugs or drinking. I understand construction in this town is pretty good. We can have a good life. Rebecca, look where you live... this is no way to raise the boys. Give me a second chance," pleaded Tony.

What could I do? I was on the verge of eviction and had nowhere to go and no one to help me. I said, "Promise me that you won't get drunk. No more hitting me and treating me like a worthless ..."

"Rebecca, I only have respect for you. It will be good. I promise. I swear to you that you and the boys will want for nothing," vowed Tony.

Josh chased Mitchell into the room both laughing. Tony picked up Mitchell and happily said, "Hey buddy, dad is back home."

I never really gave a reply. I never said yes you can come back and welcomed him with open arms. I just sat there and watched him with Mitchell. Josh however simply stood next to me and said nothing. I felt like I had no choice, it was live on the streets or let this mean bastard come back.

The trailer was real small and so privacy was none existent. Therefore, Tony simply fixed his bed on the couch that night. Dinner was Cheese cats and so the next day Tony took us to the grocery store and bought a ton of groceries. He went to the office and paid back-rent and a month ahead. Then he gave me money to pay all the utility bills. I felt like such a loser but he was being nice and civil.

That first year, I have to admit was not bad. He immediately got a job and worked long hours and Saturdays trying to build up enough money to buy a house. He kept his word and did not drink or use drugs. I did not love him but I became his wife again. Strangely, he did not really bother me for sex to my great relief.

Tony got a new truck and fixed the car and so we both had our own transportation. I began visiting Nancy. I knew she did not want me in her house but I had this desperate need to make peace with her. She never kicked me out but the insults never stopped. I was confused and exhausted with my life. I do not know what I would have done without my boys.

Within a year and a half, we were moving to our new house. It was real nice with a big backyard. It was also walking distance to an elementary school. Tony did not really know how to bond with the boys, he thought so long as he provided that was his job as husband and father. He was back in the Union now and secured himself a good job with a small company of which he made many friends.

Now that Tony had friends of which were Mexican like him, he felt at home and all his promises were now forgotten. He began drinking again and turned back into that devil who took great pleasure in tormenting me. I felt like such a failure, I could not provide for my boys on my own and now I was back to a living hell. However, my outlook was different now, this was a hell that I was simply going to accept. There would be no more dreams of escape or a better life for me. Now, I would endure to be sure all my son’s needs were met.

Chapter 20

Appearances and Dark Secrets

Life for me became a constant performance. In public, I wore a smile and appeared to be a happy housewife, devoted to my children and husband. Late at night, I was a THING for Tony to make sport of, in his never-ending need to dominate me, torture me, rape me and threaten me with death. The verbal abuse was worst than I ever experienced in my life, which is to say a lot.

His idea of a wife was strange to say the least he belittled me calling me disgusting and ugly to the extent, that it reinforced what I was taught as a child. My body was a repulsive thing to hide. I know now that he wanted to break my spirit, to keep me home without worry that I would cheat on him. Tony thought kissing was the nastiest thing two people could do, sex for him was only missionary, forced with tears of terror running down my cheeks. All the while, my torture was in complete silence so the boys would be oblivious to what went on behind a closed door.

Tony believed if a wife enjoyed sex or simply submitted to it willingly that was proof that she was sneaking out with other men. It was an insane relationship. The one good thing was we had separate bedrooms giving me a small degree of relief. To the neighbors, Tony appeared to be the perfect husband, with the perfect house and family as I wept in secret.

At times, it was unbearable when Tony came home drunk. I remember one day, I simply felt like erupting. I could not stand holding in the anger any more when Josh ran up complaining about something or other and I slapped him hard across the face leaving a bright red welt. I felt like dying on the spot as I looked at his dark soulful eyes that didn't even shed a tear, he just stood there in shock. I embraced him to my heart and told him I was sorry. I would have preferred to cut my hand off then to harm my children.

Thereby, to cope with my situation after that, I returned to drinking in secret. No one ever suspected. I was never drunk and it gave me more of a pleasant mood with my children.

Mitchell joined Karate at 7 years old and for a short time so did Josh. However, Mitchell took to it with zeal, loving every moment of it. Josh took an interest in art and writing and I happily encouraged him. My children were my life's blood, my salvation and my way of keeping my sanity.

I watched my boys grow to teenagers having nearly everything that they could want; all their needs met. I, in the meantime, developed health problems and a weight problem. I was depressed, stressed and just unhappy despite my plastic smile. It infuriated Tony to see me growing old, fat and uglier. He would go on and on about what a fat disgusting mess I turned into and that any one of his girlfriends were better than me.

I would like to pause here to say, from the time Tony returned to this point, is filled with terrible abuse, to the extent I seemed to be constantly recovering from injuries. However, he was not a complete idiot and was sure never to hurt my face and draw attention. Understand that emotionally I was broken, I had given up which I know now is typical for a battered wife. I accepted the fact that he would in fact kill me one day and all I could hope for was that the boys were grown-up when that time came so they could be on their own. Today, there are so many sources to help abused women and I sadly hear that most abused women do not take advantage of the help that is available. People do not understand to the extent that they think women like the abuse and therefore get what they deserve. It is a sad dark world for women in this position.

Now that the boys were teenagers, they did not need me as much and I thought I might like to return to school, just for fun. Infuriated Tony ranted and raved telling me I was only looking to find other men. Not realizing that Josh was in the house, Tony was surprised when Josh entered the room and said, “Let Mom go to school if she wants to. Why do you always have to be so mean to her? I am attending the Community College, she and I can go together so you can put your dirty mind to rest.”

With that said, Mitchell over heard and also came to my defense. I was so surprised and happy to see my sons stand up for me. Tony agreed but refused to pay one penny for my education saying, “Go to school then, but I am not paying for it.”

After Tony left the room, I happily thanked my boys for their support. I knew I could get a grant and so I quickly applied for it anxiously waiting for the reply. My life was taking a slight turn for the better now. I was a terrible student when I was in high school but that was then. I wanted so much to succeed at something. It took six months to get all the paper work taken care of, processed and finally the approval. I collected the check and proceeded to register for class.

Not knowing what I wanted to study I took many tests and was advised that Child Development would be a good field for me. I was so nervous my first day of class, I was 38 years old and so many of the students mistook me for the instructor. It was all so exciting. It was a big challenge but it helped me to have Josh close by, now and then, we would have lunch together or sit and talk. I studied hard, while trying to have dinner on time, the house clean and the laundry done. At the end of my first semester, I was waiting for grades to be posted. All I wanted was to pass, hoping for at least a C because less than a C and I'd lose my grant. When I received my grade report I had to sit down, tears came to my eyes as I felt beyond speech. I received a perfect score of 4.0 all A's! I could not believe it, at last a success.

I was beyond joy as I drove home. However, it was summer now and I would have to wait until the fall to return to school. Then to make matters worse Josh left for basic training, he joined the National guard. My baby was grown-up and about to begin his life.

That summer, while Josh was away Mitchell spent a good deal of time at his Karate school, as he now became the assistant and protégé to his instructor and owner of the school. My life turned back to the old ways, housekeeper and drone. I did a short fictional story as part of an English class assignment. My English teacher wrote a note on it recommending I finish the story and get it published. Published! She thought I was good enough to be a writer! My dream of which I had given up hope long ago might possibly come true.

During the day while Tony was at work, I worked on that story, revising it and reading it and enhancing the characters. By the end of summer, it was a full manuscript of 600 pages. My dream returned, somehow I would be a writer. When Josh came home, I shared with both boys about my literary dreams and as I suspected they highly encouraged me.

However, it did not meet Tony's approval, "You just want to look smarter than me. You are an idiot, fat and ugly and won't ever amount to anything. Cleaning toilets is all you can do."

Of course he said this when the boys were not present. Nevertheless, I would pursue my dream even if I had to write in secret from Tony. With all the secrets I had what was one more.

I did well in school and happily accepted a work-study program of which was the most fun I ever had. I worked in an office and learned how to use a computer. I did data entry, made appointments and answered the phone. Now and then, I would monitor a class during a test for a professor. I attended college for four years and loved my work-study program. I made friends with my fellow students and co-workers but I saw them only at school. I was forbidden to socialize outside the home without Tony and of course, he didn't ever want to socialize with me. It didn't matter, what I enjoyed during the day gave me the will to push on and succeed.

At school, nobody suspected as to what my life was like at home. I was happy as far as anyone could tell. I was a closet drinker, abused, lonely and now hiding the fact that I wanted to be a writer and therefore my life was filled with secrets.

Then, Josh told me he was moving out and wanted an apartment, a place of his own. A few months after that Mitchell fell in love and moved to Europe to study art and live with his girlfriend. My heart sank to see my boys leave me. They were everything to me. But, I happily encouraged them to follow their dreams because far be it from me to ever try to hold them back. I wanted them to experience life and enjoy it thoroughly.

Now, I was alone with Tony, he no longer had a need to try and hold back or hide how he treated me. Death threats became worst. I finished school and so I had to leave the work-study program never to see all those wonderful people again. I was back in prison and felt like death was just around the corner. Headaches, insomnia and heart palpations began to plague me, then pneumonia of which I struggled to recover. One way or another, God was trying to kill me as I saw it.

I would go to the doctor often and said my lines well, "I am just fine. The bump or bruise was because I fell. Bla bla bla." the lies spilled out of me without thought or emotion. All that mattered was appearances and keeping my dark secrets.

Chapter 21

Escape at Last!

Josh stopped by to visit me now and them but his life was filled with work and the National guard. Mitchell emailed me often from the Netherlands yet I felt that my life was beyond empty and unhappy. I dove wholeheartedly into my fantasy word, my first novel completed I wrote a second, then a third, ten in all, in an epic series. In my fantasy world, I was strong, courageous and could kill whoever got in my way. It was a bit of escape for me. I sent out my first manuscript to agents and publisher and got rejection letter after rejection letter but I did not give up. I had nothing to lose so I kept sending out query letters and sample chapters.

I sat one afternoon feeling rather melancholy when Josh arrived with his girlfriend, Olivia and announced they were getting married. Well, I was so happy for them and we immediately started discussing the wedding. A week later, I received a call from Mitchell, "Mom, I'm coming home." The joy that consumed me was beyond words.

Olivia and I went shopping and made wedding plans for July. Mitchell would be home in June with his girlfriend. How exciting, this also meant that Tony would have to control himself because his drinking had become nearly frightening. There was not a day that he was not drunk and belligerent. He would get up in the middle of the night thirsty for a beer. He started looking old and worn out as I thought he would surely die from alcoholism before long. Possibly, I could actually out live him. But it didn't look good for me; I was plagued with breathing problems and heart problems. I guess we were both dying.

When Mitchell arrived at the airport, it was such a happy reunion. As we drove home, I suggested we stop and have lunch at a restaurant. His girlfriend, Sasha was nice but I found her rather stuffy and overbearing. I said nothing, it was Mitchell's choice and all I cared about was his happiness. She was European and maybe that is just how they are.

Once home it was such a festive-occasion and Josh who had been to Europe a few times with the National Guard spoke with Mitchell about their travels. I listened and longed to travel one day. It pleased me that my sons were enjoying life to such an extent and had every opportunity to see the world.

Then, Tony walked in drunk and disgusting he could barely walk and spoke with a slur. Both Mitchell and Josh looked on with a frown probably feeling embarrassed in front of their girlfriends. Tony greeted them then proceeded to be guided to his room by Mitchell, and passed out on his bed.

Mitchell said as he closed the bedroom door, "Dad never changes."

Sasha changed the subject by showing us pictures of the travels that she and Mitchell experienced. I wore my plastic smile while fuming inside, because Tony was so embarrassing. Surprisingly over the next few weeks, Tony made no attempt to control his drinking in front of the boys and spoke to me with no regard for them or me.

On Josh's wedding day, my boys looked so handsome. Mitchell was Josh's best man; I felt my heart fill with pride. Over the few weeks prior to the wedding, I had worked on a speech for Josh, a heartfelt speech of my love for him. It was never in my nature to speak of my feelings, to express love even to my boys. The only way I could show my love was by taking care of my boys and doing whatever I could for them. But, on this special day, I wanted to open my heart up and let Josh and everyone know how much he meant to me.

At the reception when it was time for toasts and speeches, I stood up feeling quite nervous and read from my paper, the speech I worked so hard on, each word a mother's love for her son.

Everyone fell silent to listen to me when Tony shouted out in a drunken stupor, "Shut the fuck up!" I felt my heart skip a beat feeling beyond embarrassment but I refused to let him ruin this moment between me and Josh. I just kept on reading when he shouted out again, "Shut the fuck up!" Oh my god, I felt near tears but finished my speech. I embraced Josh as everyone applauded pretending they did not notice Tony's outburst.

Tony was stinking drunk and stumbling around. Mitchell became upset and tried to quite his father but to no avail. The people, who ran the reception hall, were upset with Tony's savage behavior as he insulted a waitress and I was told that he had to leave or the police would be called. I looked at my boys feeling the hatred I felt for Tony make my blood boil. The party over, we left everyone being polite and saying good night and wishing the wedding couple well.

That night as I lay in bed I thought, *Josh and Mitchell don't need me anymore. I only have to worry about myself. I don't need to put up with this shit... not anymore. I hate him! I am getting the hell out of here once and for all. I'll go far away and start a new life. I can do it!*

And so, began my plotting and planning to escape. I confided in my boys and they offered to help me. For once in my life, I had help. I needed money first and I needed to be careful and plan with patience, after all my life was on the line. I went to the bank and check to see what the saving amounted too. I never really had control of the money so I had no idea how much money we had. My god, we had $40,000 in savings! I thought, I cannot be greedy and when the time is right, I'll take $10,000. In all I had lived with that pig of a man for nearly 30 years and I would walk away with nothing but $10,000, I didn't care about the house, its contents or the property we owned. He could have it all. I just wanted my freedom.

Together, my boys and I planned on where I would move to, I had to go far. Well, Sasha was now going to Portland to do an internship as a microbiologist. Therefore, it was agreed that would be a good place to go because at least I would have Mitchell close by and won't be entirely alone. I was real excited about my newest secret.

That evening Mitchell and Josh took their girls out on the town. I was home watching TV when Tony walked in looking like an angry thundercloud. I tried to be calm and not say anything. I hurried and served him a plate of dinner and tried to do all the right things so he would not hurt me. He sat down and stared at me then said, "I can kill you right now, take you into the back yard, cut you up, take you out to the desert and scatter your body parts for the coyotes to eat. Look at you, you have grey hair and look like a pig."

I sat perfectly still and offered no reply because I knew if I said anything, he would go crazy. He stood up and paced them told me, "Tell me the truth... you have a boyfriend don't you?"

Surprised, I replied, "No. Why do you ask such a thing?"

He glared at me then said, "Tell me the truth

I want to hear the truth... you want to leave me don't you? Just say it. I am happy to hear the truth."

Again surprised, I thought for a moment maybe he wants to leave me and is looking for me to make the first move. So, like a dumb ass I replied, "Yes, I want divorce. You can keep everything, the house, the property, everything. You don't have to pay me alimony or anything."

I was so relived to say the words to him when all hell broke loose. He looked at me with murder in his eyes as he went for a kitchen knife. "I am going to cut you to pieces. I keep everything that is mind... even the junk. You are going nowhere."

He came at me and I ran to my bedroom like an idiot instead of the front door. I grabbed the phone and dialed 911. He shouted at me, "Put the phone down. Who are you calling?"

I hung up the phone and realized this was it he was going to kill me. He looked at me and I looked at him for a moment when the phone rang. Tony grabbed the phone and replied with a calm voice, "Nothing's wrong. My wife is a little crazy. There is nothing to worry about." He hung up the phone and took a step closer to me, "How dare you call the cops. Tomorrow morning I will tell the boys you ran off with your lover and didn't care about them or me. I am..."

Suddenly, there was pounding at the door. Then I heard, "Open the door, this is the police." I ran passed Tony and to the front door where a police officer grabbed my hand and pulled me outside. Another officer went into the house. A female police officer asked me, "What happened, are you all right?" I explained to the letter what happened and the threats Tony made with knife in hand.

I do not know what they said to Tony but apparently, they could not arrest him because he did not hurt me. I was panic stricken for them to leave me alone with him and expressed my fears to the police. All the cops left except the female and her partner, they waited with me until the boys came home and ordered Tony to stay in his bedroom. He did, as he was told not making a fuss to be sure, I looked like a fool.

The boys entered the house a half hour later. Normally Josh would have just dropped Mitchell off but when he saw the police car, he went in to see what was happening. Mitchell looked in Tony's room then came over to me and said, "He's asleep, or passed out."

I thanked the police for staying with me and that night Olivia insisted that I go home with them for my safety. I quickly packed a bag, got my cat and went to Josh's apartment. It was the turning point in my life. I could never go back, ever. The next day, early in the morning Tony called and Josh told him I was staying with him and not going back home.

Three days later Olivia and I went to the bank where I withdrew $10,000. The day after that right after Tony went to work, Josh, Mitchell, Sasha and Olivia helped me pack my car with my personal possession. I was in a panic not sure what to take and what to leave. We were there a couple of hours then drove off.

I flew to Portland and spent a week there looking for an apartment then returned to Las Vegas, where I said farewell to Josh and Olivia. Sasha flew ahead to Portland to prepare for her internship and Mitchell and I drove to Portland. On the road, I turned the radio on and a song played the lyrics, “I don’t care what you say this is my life, leave me alone.”

It happened I was free, free. It took us three days to reach Portland staying at motels at night and taking in the sights. I was so happy feeling a heavy weight lifted off my shoulders. I had a college degree now and some experience of life. I would survive and make my mark on the world. I would be a famous writer one day and make all my dreams come true.

Chapter 22

If I Can Do It Anyone Can Do It

From the time, I was four years old until I was nearly fifty years old; I was terribly abused and lost all sense of pride. I had no self-esteem, feeling abandoned by god. Now as I look back, I feel I must share my experiences with those women who grew up abused and then fell to the hands of an abusive husband. I spent nearly all my adult years to please others. I became a closet drinker, depressed and emotionless. Physical affection never came natural to me, not even toward my sons. Touching, caressing, kissing and words of endearment were foreign to me. I certainly did not know how to return love. I was and I guess still am uncomfortable with my body and appearance.

Do not make the mistakes I did by keeping secrets and lying to protect your abuser. When I finally had enough and mentioned to a few people that I was leaving Tony to divorce him they were shocked. Because I always pretended that my life was wonderful and that Tony was a good husband, thereby people could not understand why I would leave him. I looked like the bad-guy. Many believed I simply abandoned Tony with no regards for his feelings. I could never explain it because nobody would believe me at such a late date, to come forward with a lengthy history of abuse. I suppose many still think I am nuts, selfish and unappreciative.

Do not keep secrets, tell people that you are in trouble; welfare, the police, neighbors, family, friends and doctors. Show them your bruises and tell the truth about what happened. It will save your life and free you from your torment. Do not be afraid to try and make it on your own, even if you have small children. There is always welfare, do not refuse help.

Finally, I made it on my own but it was not easy. I got a job, paid my bills and learned to breathe free air. Never will I allow myself to be abused again. I worked for a while as a pre-school teacher. It felt so good to go to my own apartment, my personal space where I did not have to answer to anyone. True, I was a little afraid at night being all alone, never had I been alone in my entire life. I began to go out to movies and now and then Mitchell would visit me. I even went out on occasions with co-workers and had a great time.

After two years on my own, I met the man of my dreams. William is so charming, so loving and attentive. We travel, take cruises and spend every day just taking care of each other. He restored my faith in god. I am a worthwhile person who matters and my beloved husband always insures that I understand that. Today, I am a published author, another dream come true. Goes to show it is never too late to make your dreams come true.

On a final note, I want to say I never got the peace I wanted between me and Nancy, in fact, things got even worst between us and we simply disconnected. The last time I saw her, her words to me were, “I am done with you... I consider you dead!” I left and five years later, I received a phone call late one night informing me that Nancy passed away. Yes, I did shed tears, she was my mother after all and it hurt me deeply that we never had peace between us. I made every attempt to be a good daughter to her, my conscious is clear and now she has to deal with her demons. I suffer from deep emotional scares but I learned not to let myself fall to depression and I do not drink anymore.

Happiness is my purpose now. I was relieved when I heard that Tony remarried, that meant he gave up and let me go...he is no longer part of my life. My boys are and always have been my salvation and now I have a granddaughter to love. As I look back, I could have always done it on my own. I was a fool not to go to Welfare when I needed it. This is a wonderful country and offers us many options. No one needs to be oppressed or to suffer abuse. We all have a right to be safe and free.

Life is good and it can be for you too. Take advantage of the government services for abused women. There are shelters that will protect you, do not feel embarrassed to go for help and do not keep your situation a secret, get out while you can.

Poem:

My name is Rebecca

but at home they call me Rebecca Marie. I am but a thin rail of a girl, not much of me. My eyes are swollen and I cannot see, my mother hit me because I'm so clumsy. I must be stupid, I must be bad, what else could have made mommy so mad?

Or, is it just that she hates me because I am her shame? She took a man of color for greed without a care and as a result I have black hair. My eyes are a dark mirror of her error, my skin not fair and I stutter and stutter. Dummy she calls me, I am no good . . . a product of evil . . .
Her shame, her weakness, her terrible trouble. I wish I were better, I wish I weren't ugly, I wish I was fair. Oh how I wish her equal I could be, then, maybe my Mommy would want to hug me.

I can't speak at all. I can't do a wrong or else I'm locked up all the day long. No food for my belly, no warmth for my bones, just a dark cold corner to call my own.

When I awake I feel alone, till the spirits of children come to comfort me and make me feel a reason to be. Is it real or my mind that is lost to seek out those innocent souls who understand my pain . . . having died by the same.

When my Mommy comes, I'll try and be nice, So maybe I'll get just one whipping tonight. Maybe, just maybe I can have a dinner plate or maybe just maybe I can come in tonight . . .
Out of the cold dark corner of my cell where only the spiders dwell.

Don't make a sound! I just heard a car. I hear her curse . . . My name she calls . . . I press myself against the wall. I try and hide from her evil eyes. I am so afraid now I'm starting to cry.

She finds me weeping . . . she shouts ugly words; she says it's my fault that she suffers at work. I am her shame and the neighbors will see that I am much less than I should be.

She slaps me and hits me and yells at me more. I finally get free and run for the door. She's already locked it and I start to bawl, she takes me and throws me against the hard wall.

I fall to the floor, with my bones nearly broken, as my mommy continues with more bad words spoken.

"I'm sorry!" I scream. But, it's now too late her face

has twisted to unimaginable hate.

The hurt and the pain, again and again. Oh please God, have mercy! Oh, please let it end!

She finally stops, and heads for the door, while I lay there motionless, sprawled on the floor.

My name is Rebecca but at home they call me Rebecca Marie and my mommy hates me.
I am not included . . . I don't belong . . . my daddy has left me at the hands of this shark. Why did he leave me? Why did he go? How could he do it when he loves me so?

In the garage, I hear from within my mommy's perfect home, her perfect children happy in song . . . where I am not wanted where I don't belong . . .
to her she's not mommy . . . to me . . .
I can only call her Nancy.

I hope you enjoyed reading my story and possibly, it can help you heal if you had a similar experience. Or, hopefully it enlightened you as to abuse and thereby opens the door for you to help someone in need.

I dedicate this book to social workers who deserve applause and to women who need to find the footing to leave their dangerous situation. I also dedicate this book to the children and woman who did not survive their abuse.

Made in the USA
Lexington, KY
28 February 2011